Bladen County North Carolina

Tax Lists

1768 through 1774

Volume I

William L. Byrd, III

Heritage Books
2025

HERITAGE BOOKS

AN IMPRINT OF HERITAGE BOOKS, INC.

Books, CDs, and more—Worldwide

For our listing of thousands of titles see our website
at
www.HeritageBooks.com

Published 2025 by
HERITAGE BOOKS, INC.
Publishing Division
5810 Ruatan Street
Berwyn Heights, MD 20740

Library of Congress Catalogue Number: 98-073646

International Standard Book Number
Paperbound: 978-0-9667425-0-3

ACKNOWLEDGEMENTS

The publishing of this book would not have been possible without the help and encouragement of various individuals. Formost I would to express my sincere gratitude to Richard Shrader, Reference Archivist, for the Southern Historical Collection at the University of North Carolina, and his staff. They patiently and consistently brought manuscript boxes to me, and reserved them overnight so I could begin again first thing the next morning. They answered my many questions (some meaningful and some not so meaningful) promptly and courteously. All in all, they made it a pleasant place to spend a few weeks. Permission has also been granted by the Southern Historical Collection of the University of North Carolina to publish these transcriptions.

I also must express my undying gratitude to Jo White Linn (a dear and valuable friend) of Salisbury, North Carolina. I probably would not have published this book without her encouragement. She offered her knowledge of publishing and made suggestions that improved the quality of this volume. She gave me a few gentle shoves when I needed it the most. Reluctant as I am, I followed her suggestions, and it has made all the difference in this project. I simply cannot thank her enough.

Lastly, I dedicate this book to my two grandsons William Paul Huffman and Miguel Esteban Byrd, who have been a never ending source of inspiration to me.

INTRODUCTION

Bladen County was formed from New Hanover Precinct in 1734. At this time it existed as a precinct of Bath County. In 1800 and 1893 Courthouse fires destroyed most of Bladen's court records and some of the land deeds.[1] The devastation of Bladen County's records by these fires has created a void for historians and genealogists alike. These early tax lists provide information and insight into many of the early families that would have otherwise been lost to posterity. Several of the lists gives the names of sons and servants and in some cases they list the names of other relatives. Many of the wives are listed in free mixed blood families and a myriad of slave's names abound throughout the lists.

When Bladen County was first formed it covered a large territory from which other counties eventually came into existence. Anson County was formed in 1750 from Bladen, and part of Orange County was formed from Bladen in 1752. In 1754 Cumberland County was formed from Bladen, and later, in 1764, Brunswick County was formed from Bladen and New Hanover County. Twenty three years later, in 1787, Robeson County was formed from Bladen.[2]

The Bladen County records in this volume were obtained from the *Thomas David Smith McDowell Papers*. They are a part of the vast collection housed in the *Southern Historical Collection* at the Wilson Library of the University of North Carolina. There are 3000 items and five volumes contained in this collection alone.

Many of the tax lists included in this volume are incomplete. Some are torn and others are missing pages. Quite a few of the lists are in a severe state of deterioration and had to be transcribed from the originals rather than from copies. Within the 1774 lists is a complete county wide register that has provided some accurate statistics of Bladen County for that year. See Appendix C for statistics.

This volume contains tax lists for the years 1768-1774. A proposed second volume (in progress at this time) will consist of the tax lists of 1775 through 1789, and a good number of loose papers that will be complete transcriptions. There is enough information in these records to shed new light on an otherwise burned county. This volume should be of interest to historians, statisticians, and genealogists alike.

Old Bladen County was also home to many of the ancestral families of the Lumbee Indian Tribe of North Carolina. They will be found listed variously as Whites, Mulattoes, and Mixt Bloods. Bound together by a common ancestry, they have survived to this day as a unified group. Their mark has been indelibly stamped on North Carolina's history. Included in this volume is a 1773 petition from the General Assembly Sessions Records (See Appendix B) referring to a group of them who banded together, and were living illegally on the King's land.

Free Persons of Color are listed in italics in the various tax lists in this volume. It should be of note that the wives and other females in this group are given as taxables. This policy originated from a statute passed by the General Assembly in 1723 as a result of so many mixed blood people who were moving into the colony and intermarrying with Whites. Inter-racial marriages were forbidden by an earlier statute passed by the General Assembly in 1715. This same statute was again confirmed in 1741. The statute of 1723 wherein mixed bloods and their wives and daughters were both considered taxables was again confirmed in 1749

In 1755 a petition was submitted to the General Assembly praying relief from the 1723 statute, but no results came from it. Five years later, in 1760, an act passed by the General Assembly again reaffirmed

---

[1] *Guide to Research Materials in the North Carolina State Archives: County Records,* eleventh rev. ed. (Raleigh: Division of Archives and History, Department of Cultural Resources, 1997): 31.

[2] David Leroy Corbit, *The Formation of the North Carolina Counties: 1663-1943* (1950; reprint, Raleigh: Division of Archives and History, Department of Cultural Resources, 1987): 27-31.

the 1723 statute. This resulted in another petition being filed with the General Assembly in 1762 by sundry inhabitants of several North Carolina Counties protesting the paying of taxes on their wives and daughters. This statute, however, remained on the books, and Free Persons of Color were still paying taxes on their wives and daughters in 1774. See Appendix A for the actual laws and petitions.

It should also be noted that Patrollers were also exempt from taxes. The first statute defining Patrollers (or Searchers) was enacted by the General Assembly in 1753. This statute gave the Patrollers broad powers to search slaves and their quarters for guns, swords, clubs, or any other weapons. See Appendix A for the 1753 statute.

Another confusion factor for Bladen County stems from a border problem with South Carolina. This problem was adressed in a *Guide to South Carolina Genealogical Research and Records* by Brent Holcomb.

> The North Carolina-South Carolina border east of the Catawba River was surveyed in 1764, and west of the Catawba River in 1772. Prior to these surveys, much of the territory in the north-central and north-western part of South Carolina was considered to be North Carolina. The South Carolina counties of Marlboro, Chesterfield, Lancaster, York, Chester, Union, Spartanburg, Cherokee, and portions of Greenville, Laurens and Newberry are involved. There are three, or in some cases, four North Carolina counties to be considered: Bladen ca. 1745-1749, Anson 1749-1764, Mecklenburg 1763-1772, and Tryon 1769-1772. The researcher should consider persons in that area as though they were residents of North Carolina and search the appropriate records in that state:[3]

Considering the above excerpt, the tax lists in this volume should be of interest to North Carolina and South Carolina researchers alike. Adjacent border research (especially across state lines) has routinely been overlooked by many researchers.

---

[3] Brent Howard Holcomb, *A Guide to South Carolina Genealogical Research and Records* (Privately printed, 1986): 39.

TABLE OF CONTENTS

Mouzon 1775 (W.P. Cumming, *North Carolina in Maps (1966)*, Plate VIII

A Quest And True List of The
Masters and Mistresses of Every
Family & Overseers of Every Plantation
Within my District

Thos Amis
Joshua Stevens
Jacob Harchy
John Butler
Luke Mansfield
William Boyit
Gabriel Parker
Michael Whitman
Dempsey Dawson
William Strickland
Moses Coleman
Coleman Nichols
John Yates
Nehemiah Johnston
John Rogers
Edward Wilson
John Branton
Ignatious Flowers
Kirkly Hays

Summoned to give in their List of Taxables Before
Mr John Turner,   Ten Days Before Neat Court
By me   Jno Coleman

Summond in Henry Boswell's District

Abraham King
Joseph Noss
James Wilson   By me — Jno Coleman
David Clark
Simon Bright
William   Boyces
David Godwin   June ye 29. 1775

Bladen County Tax List, 1775

CHAPTER 1

BLADEN COUNTY TAX LISTS OF 1768

PARTIAL BLADEN COUNTYTAX LIST OF 1768

Headings for this list include: White Men, Male Slaves, Female Slaves, Boys, & In All

White Men	
Thomas Johnson	1
Solomon Johnson	1
Zachariah Dyson	1
Male Slaves July	1
In All	4

White Men	
Thomas Dyson	1
In All	1

White Men	
Nehemiah Johnson	1
In All	1

White Men	
John Willson Senr	1
James Willson	1
In All	2

White Men	
David Morley	1
Male Slaves	2
Will, Cudjoe	
In All	3

White Men	
William Johnson	1
John Johnson	1
In All	2

White Men	
Barnaba Stevens	1
William Stevens	1
Male Slaves	2
Aro, Aberdeen	
Female Slaves	1
Diana	
In All	5

White Men	
Isum S[?]ehen	1
In All	1

White Men	
Peregrine Johnson	1
In All	1

White Men	
Isaac Stephens	1
In All	1

White Men	
John Johnson	1
In All	1

White Men	
Cloud Cunningham	1
In All	1

White Men	
Edward Wall	1
In All	1

White Men	
John Baldwin Jr.	1
Male Slaves	1
Quash	
In All	2

White Men	
James Money	1
In All	1

White Men	
John Willson Jur.	1
In All	1

White Men	
William Lewis	1
In All	1

White Men	
Thomas Saunders	1
William Saunders	1
Female Slaves	1
Frances	
In All	3

White Men	
Christphr Saunders	1
In All	1

White Men	
Danl. McNicholds	1
William Robinson	1
In All	2

White Men	
David Duncan	1
In All	1

White Men	
Caleb Callaway	1
In All	1

White Men	
Bendick Williams	1
In All	1

White Men	
Thomas Boon	1
William Boon	1
John Boon	1
In All	3

White Men	
George Clark	1
Henry Lambethion	1
In All	2

White Men	
Edward Willson	1
In All	1

White Men	
John Braxton	1
In All	1

White Men	
William Adams	1
Benjamin Adams	1
In All	2

White Men	
Balither Hays	1
In All	1

White Men	
John Linsey	1
In All	1

White Men	
Benjamin Baskin	1
In All	1

White Men	
James Farrier	1
In All	1

White Men	
Daniel Flinn	1
William Robins	1
In All	2

White Men	
Alexander Stevens	1
In All	1

White Men	
Edmund Ruark	1
Male Slaves	1
Ceasar	
In All	2

White Men	
Edward Searcy	1
Michael Morell	1
Ezekle Hill	1
Male Slaves	1
Joshua	
In All	4

White Men	
John Baker	1
John Simpson	1
Female Slaves	1
Jane	
In All	3

White Men	
Robert Hatcher	1
In All	1

White Men	
Southy Hays	1
Richard Shephard	1
In All	2

White Men	
John Buzby	1
In All	1

Chapter 1:   Bladen County Tax Lists of 1768

<table>
<tr><td>

White Men
Henry Sutton — 1
In All — 1

White Men
John McCoy — 1
In All — 1

White Men
John Williams — 1
In All — 1

White Men
Richard Bigges Jr — 1
Female Slaves — 1
Mary
In All — 2

White Men
John Green — 1
In All — 1

White Men
Abraham King — 1
In All — 1

White Men
Danel Corbet — 1
In All — 1

White Men
John [Faded] — 1
In All — 1

White Men
Isaac Stephens — 1
In All — 1

White Men
William [Faded] — 1
In All — 1

White Men
George Gibbs — 1
Benjamin Nail — 1
Male Slaves — 6
Tony, Jamy, Kent, Walley, Jack, patrick
Female Slaves — 5
Betty, Dina, Hanna, Bella, Minda, Sabina
Boys — 1
Jemmy
In All — 14

</td><td>

White Men
Joshua Stevens — 1
Male Slaves — 1
Peter
Female Slaves — 2
Brenda, Vilate
In All — 4

White Men
James Cunningham — 1
In All — 1

****

BLADEN COUNTY TAX LIST OF 1768

An Exact List of [Torn] by me

A True List of Taxables for the Year 1768 by me Archd. McKissack

Headings for this list include: Whites, Blacks, Mulatoes, & No.

Whites
James macdwel [Torn] — 1
No. — 1

Whites
Joseph Mercer & Lot Mercer
No. — 2

Whites
William Lewis — 1
No. — 1

Whites
John macGregor — 1
No. — 1

Whites
Reubin Roberts — 1
Blacks — 1
Fellow Jack
No. — 2

Whites
David Growter — 1
No. — 1

Whites
Samuel andrew & son Sam — 2

No. — 2

</td></tr>
</table>

Whites
John Carpenter 1
No. _____

Whites
Demsy & Charles Bairfield & John Cross 3
No. _____ 3

Whites
John Odom & son William 2
No. _____ 2

Whites
Thos. Odom & Barnabas Lamb 2
Blacks 1
Negroe wench dicy
Mulatoes 1
Isom Skipper
No. _____ 4

Whites
James Cook 1
No. _____ 1

Whites
Aaron Odom & Silas Adkins & William
Lettamer [?] and James Snowden 4
No. _____ 4

Mulatoes 1
Arthur Lamb
No. _____ 1

Whites
Jonathan Taylor 1
No. _____ 1

Whites
Samson Taylor 1
No. _____ 1

Whites
Henry Tayler 1
No. _____ 1

Whites
Benjamin Ivey 1
No. _____ 1

Mulatoes 2
Simon Cox & adam Ivey
No. _____ 2

Whites
Thos. Brown & two sons Edmond & Thomas
3
No. _____ 3

Whites
Benjamin Odom 1
Mulatoes 1
William Wilkins
No. _____ 2

Whites
David Bairfield 1
No. _____ 1

Whites
John Jones 1
No. _____ 1

Whites
Abraham Paul 1
No. _____ 1

Whites
Daniel & John mcLaine & Peter Jackson 3
No. _____ 3

Whites
Joseph Milton 1
No. _____ 1

Whites
Jacob Pittman 1
No. _____ 1

Whites
George Parsons 1
No. _____ 1

Whites
Christopher Garlington & Miles Bairfield 2
No. _____ 2

Whites
Daniel mudic 1
Mulatoes 1
Rasses[?] Goen
No. _____ 2

Whites
Malcolm mcNeil 1
No. _____ 1

Mulatoes 1
Thomas Cairsey Junr.
No. _____ 1

Mulatoes   1
Aaron Drake
No. _____ 1

Mulatoes   2
Ishmael Cheves & wife
No. _____ 2
Whites
Drewery fryer & Jacob Odom   2

No. _____ 2

Mulatoes   1
[Torn] [Torn]on
No. _____ 1

Whites
[Torn] [Torn]conl. & son   2
No. _____ 2

Mulatoes   5
[Torn] [Torn] & wife & son William &
daughters Sarah & Elizabeth
No. _____ 5

Whites
Jacob Alford & Samuel Haines   2
No. _____ 2

Mulatoes   2
Cannon Cumbo & wife
No. _____ 2

Whites
Roager Bairfield   1
No. _____ 1

Mulatoes   2
James Carter & son Isaac
No. _____ 2

Whites
James Wilkinson   1
No. _____ 1

Whites
John Richardson   1
No. _____ 1

Mulatoes   4
James Lowry & wife: Jas. Harpe & William
Jones
No. _____ 4

Mulatoes   1
Cudworth Oxendine
No. _____ 1

Whites
Thomas Proctor   1
No. _____ 1

Whites
Thomas Law[?]   1
No. _____ 1

Whites
Joseph fort & William Hubbard   2
Blacks   5
Negroe fellow Jacob & harry & wenches Judy:
Moll & Patt
No. _____ 7

Whites
Jesee Bagget   1
No. _____ 1

Whites
Ambrose powell   1
No. _____ 1

Whites
George young Junr.   1
No. _____ 1

Whites
John & Edmond Baxely   2
No. _____ 2

Whites
William Baxely   1
No. _____ 1

Whites
William Ard   1
No. _____ 1

Mulatoes   2
James Clark & wife
No. _____ 2

Mulatoes   2
Cooper Clark & wife
No. _____ 2

Mulatoes   1
Thomas Britt an Indian James Stewart Senr.
                                                   1
Blacks   1
Charles Valentine a free
Negroe
No.   2

Whites
Edward Flower   1
No.   1

Whites
Thos. & Jesse Pittman   2
No.   2

Whites
Thos. Muselwhite & son Milbee   2
No.   2

Whites
Jesee Muselwhite   1
No.   1

Whites
David Roazer Junr.   1
No.   1

Whites
Isaac Roazer & son William   2
No.   2

Whites
John Cairsey   1
Blacks   1
A negroe wench abie
No.   2

Whites
William Moore   1
No.   1

Whites
Thos. Jackson English   1
No.   1

Whites
William Brantly   1
No.   1

Whites
Shadrach Lee & father   2
No.   2

Whites
Vincent Roazer   1
No.   1

Whites
Daniel Willis, John Clyburn Shadrach [?],
William Willis   4
Blacks   2
Two Negroe fellows sam & York
No.   6

Whites
Hardy Inman   1
No.   1

Whites
John Blunt & sons Jacob James & Philip Blunt
and Aaron Baxely   5
No.   5

Whites
James Bagget   1
No.   1

Whites
Shadrach Bagget   1
No.   1

Whites
Thomas Ivey   1
No.   1

Whites
Joseph Bagget   1
No.   1

Whites
Nathan & Absalom Horne   2
No.   2

Mulatoes   3
Jas. Doyal & wife & Arthur Evans
No.   3

Whites
Joseph Rigan & son John   2
Blacks   3
Negroe fellow Quaco two Wenches Patience &
Luce
No.   5

Whites
Ralph Rigan   1
No.   1

Whites
John Roazer   1
No.   1

Whites
Lazarus Creal as Conl. & Son Thomas Creal
                                                          2
No.   2

Whites
Robert Ferrel   1
Blacks   2
A fellow Harry & Wench Grace
No.   3

Whites
Henry Bird & sonWilliam Bird   2
No.   2

Mulatoes   1
John Wilson
No.   1

Mulatoes   1
Solomon James
No.   1

Mulatoes   2
Moses Walker & wife
No.   2

Mulatoes   1
Thomas Russel
No.   1

Whites
Abram Barnes   1
Blacks   1
A negroe boy Jack
No.   2

Whites
Henry Cross & William Clyburn   2
No.   2

Whites
Richard [Faded]   1
No.   1

Mulatoes   2
Isaac Lamb & son Needham
No.   2

Mulatoes   3
Daniel Wharton & wife &   Son Richard Wharton
No.   3

Whites
Peter mcCarter   1
No.   1

Whites
John mcfarshon & son Daniel   2
Blacks   3
Negroe fellow Charly & two Wenches Patt & Nanny
No.   5

Whites
William Wilkinson   1
No.   1

Whites
Charles Thomson   1
No.   1

Charles oxendine Refused to Give in after he Put his hand to the Book & is two years a Defaulting before he is mixt Blood.

Mulatoes   1
Isaac Johnston
No.   1

Mulatoes   2
Jacob Lockliar & wife
No.   2

Whites
John Fiveash & son Demsey & John Paul   3
No.   3

Mulatoes   4
Joshua Purkins & two sons & wife
No.   4

Mulatoes   2
William Sweat & son Benj.
No.   2

Mulatoes   1
Joseph Ivey
No.   1

Whites
Major Lockliar   1
No.   1

Whites
Elias Horne 1
No. 1

Whites
John Dunbar 1
No. 1

Whites
John Britt 1
No. 1

Whites
[Torn] young 1
No. 1

Mulatoes 2
Joshua Braveboy & son Lewis
No. 2

Mulatoes 2
Solomon Johnston Junr. & Wife
No. 2

Whites
James [?]iyder Johnson[?] 1
No. 1

Mulatoes 1
Thomas Sweat
No. 1

Whites
Elizabeth Bess & her sons Archelaus & Bryan
2
No. 2

Whites
Thomas Baxely 1
No. 1

Whites
William Brumble 1
No. 1

Whites
Joseph Oates & son Carraway 2
Blacks 1
A Negroe fellow Antony
No. 3

Blacks
Ignatious flower 1
No. 1

Whites
Bedredon Carroway 1
No. 1

Whites
Josiah Tayler & David Page 2
No. 2

Whites
Lewis hall & two sons Isaac & Enoch & Natt:
Sanders 4
No. 4

Whites
William Hall & son William & Heigh Lewis
sanders 3
No. 3

Whites
Solomon Whitley & John Stevens 2
No. 2

Whites
Philomon Terrel & [Faded] 2
No. 2

Mulatoes 1
Gilbert Cox
No. 1

Whites
Willis finckley & his father Thos. Finckley &
Charles Finckley 3
Blacks 3
Two fellows Jo & Bains & a wench Cate
No. 6

Mulatoes 2
Peter Cairsey & son David
No. 2

Mulatoes 2
Richd. Jones & wife
No. 2

Whites
Martha Sparkman
John Rial 1
Blacks 1
A negroe wench Venus
No. 2

Whites
Jesee Moss   1
Mulatoes   1
Thomas Cairsey Senr.
No.   2

Whites
Richd. Smith   1
Blacks   1
A negroe wench Clo
No.   2

Whites
Moses Hodge   1
No.   1

Whites
Moses Grice   1
No.   1

Whites
Green obodyford   1
No.   1

Whites
Meredith Ellzey   1
No.   1

Whites
William & Ben Freeman   2
No.   2

Mulatoes   1
Moses Skipper
No.   1

Whites
Duncan Campbell   1
Blacks   1
A fellow
No.   2

Whites
Jas. [Torn]
No.   6

Whites
[Torn]   1
No.   1

Whites
Solomon Mercer & son Solomon   2
Blacks   1
Negroe fellow Limerick
No.   3

Whites
John Bullard   1
No.   1

Whites
James Stewart   1
No.   1

****

BLADEN COUNTY TAX LIST OF 1768

A List of Taxables taken by George Gibbs for the Year one Thousand seven Hundred and Sixty Eight

Headings for this list include: White Men, Negro Men, Negro Women, Boys & In All

White Men
John Gibbs   1
Negro Men   8
Ceasar, Peter, Sampson, Johney, Dennis, Barton, Tom Beck, Tom Freeman
Negro Women   7
Boatswain, Amelia, Juba, Betty, Hannah, Judey, Nan
In All   16

White Men
John Turner Esqr., [Torn]as Lovet   2
Negro Men   5
London, Solomon, Ryal, Will, Hannabal
Negro Women   4
Patience, Jane, Sarah, Grace
In All   11

White Men
Thomas Mims, David Mims   2
Negro Men   1
Tom
In All   3

White Men
[Torn]miah Bigford, [Torn]iah Bigford, [Torn] Bigford   3
Negro Women   1
Affey
In All   4

White Men
Jesse Lancaster   1
In All   1

Chapter 1:   Bladen County Tax Lists of 1768

White Men
William White — 1
Negro Men — 1
Quaco
In All — 2

White Men
William Burney, William Burney Jr. — 2
Negro Men — 1
Sam
Negro Women — 2
Jane, Pat
In All — 5

White Men
John Powell, Absalom Powell — 2
Negro Men — 2
Cyrus, Tom
In All — 4

White Men
Benjamin Lambethson, [Torn] Lambethson — 2
Negro Men — 1
Jack
Negro Women — 4
Hannah, Sarah, Jane, Doll
In All — 7

White Men
[Torn] Baldwin, [Torn] Baldwin, [Torn] Baldwin — 3
Negro Men — 1
Dublin
Negro Women — 2
Sarah & Bettey
In All — 6

White Men
[Torn] Huse, [Torn] Huse, Malachi Huse — 3
In All — 3

White Men
William Bryan — 1
Negro Men — 1
Jack
In All — 2

White Men
Jacob Norton — 1
In All — 1

White Men
James Murphey — 1
In All — 1

White Men
[Torn] Bright — 1
In All — 1

White Men
[Torn] Walker — 1
In All — 1

White Men
[Torn] Bryan — 1
In All — 1

White Men
[Torn] McClaren, [Torn] McClaren — 2
Negro Women — 1
Phebe
In All — 3

White Men
[Torn] Stuart — 1
In All — 1

White Men
Daniel Shipman, [Torn] Shipman — 2
Negro Men — 2
Ceasar, Sam
In All — 4

White Men
[Torn] Wiggans, [Torn] Wiggans — 2
In All — 2

White Men
Simon Burney — 1
In All — 1

White Men
[Torn] Ruark — 1
In All — 1

White Men
John Ellis Jr. — 1
In All — 1

White Men
Neil McCoulsky, Neil Shaw, Charles McNaughton — 3
Negro Women — 1
Phillis
Boys — 1
Charles
In All — 5

Chapter 1:   Bladen County Tax Lists of 1768

White Men
Joshua Hays   1
Negro Men   1
Tom
In All   2

White Men
Isaac Green, Jurin Routs   2
Negro Men   6
Tom, Jupiter, Quaco, Greenwich, Ceasar, Jack,
 Rubin
Negro Women   4
Betty, Chloe, Venus, Celia
In All   12

White Men
John McCune, Robert McCune, William
McCune   3
In All   3

White Men
John Conaly   1
In All   1

White Men
Jeremiah Draper   1
In All   1

White Men
David Clark   1
In All   1

White Men
John Cooke   1
In All   1

White Men
Daniel King   1
In All   1

White Men
John Baldwin, Charles Baldwin   2
Negro Men   3
[Torn], [Torn], [Torn]
Negro Women   3
Pegg, Abb, Phebe
In All   8

White Men
John Raybon, Ezekil Hull   2
In All   2

White Men
Jeremiah Brown   1
In All   1

White Men
John Green, William Green   2
Negro Men   2
Tom, Dick
Negro Women   1
Tamar
In All   5

White Men
Alexander Howell   1
In All   1

White Men
John Hilliard, James Hilliard, John Hilliard Jr.
                                                 3
In All   3

White Men
Peter Simpson   1
Negro Men   1
Joe
In All   2

White Men
Samuel Hider   1
In All   1

White Men
James Lewis, Solomon Lewis   2
In All   2

White Men
Matthew Kelly   1
Negro Men   2
Greenwich, Will
Negro Women   1
Jude
In All   4

White Men
Maurice Biven, Thomas
Jones   2
In All   2

White Men
John Ellis Snr., Robert Ellis, William Ellis   3
Negro Men   2
Dick, Lawrence
Negro Women   2
Venus, Beck
In All   7

White Men
Josias Lewis, John Simpson   2
Negro Men   1
In All   3

White Men
Daniel Norton, Richard Mullington   2
In All   2

White Men
Archd. McCoulsky, James McCoulsky   2
Negro Women   1
Chloe
In All   3

White Men
Daniel Shaw   1
Negro Men   1
Ben
Negro Women   1
Phebe
In All   3

White Men
Handson Lewis, Josiah Lewis   2
Negro Men   1
Will
Negro Women   1
Patt
In All   4

White Men
William McNeilson   1
Negro Men   3
Duncan, Mercury, Camblton
Negro Women   2
Chloe, Venus
In All   6

White Men
Saml. Etheridge, Jon Etheridge, Marmdk.
Etheridge, Hos[?] Steurt   4
Negro Women   2
Chloe, Venus
In All   6

White Men
Berryman Watts   1
In All   1

White Men
Richd. Ridgett Snr.   1
In All   1

White Men
John Stubbs, Richard Stubbs   2
In All   2

White Men
Thos. Richardson   1
In All   1

White Men
Joseph Sims, James Sims   2
In All   2

White Men
Peter Dubose   1
In All   1

White Men
Zachariah Smith, James Green   2
Negro Men   1
Dick
In All   3

White Men
James Ker[?]   1
Negro Men   1
Tony
In All   2

White Men
John Chancey   1
Negro Men   1
Frank
Negro Women   2
Grace, Sue
In All   4

White Men
Daniel Turner   1
In All   1

White Men
Darby Murphey, John McClaren   2
In All   2

White Men
Daniel Bahoon[?]   1
In All   1

Negro Women   1
Susanna Freeman
Negro Men   3
Abraham Freeman, Saml. Freeman, Roger
Freeman
[This group are most likely free Negroes] In
All   4

CHAPTER 2

BLADEN COUNTY TAX LISTS OF 1769

BLADEN COUNTY TAX LIST OF 1769

A True List of taxables for the yr. 1769 taken

Taken by me Archd. MKissack J:P List of Taxables for 1769 Total 321

Headings for this list include: White, Black, Mulatoes, & No.

White	
Peter McCarter	1
No.	1
Whites	
Lewis munrow	1
No.	1
Whites	
Malcolm munrow	1
No.	1
Whites	
Joseph Mercer	1
No.	1
Whites	
Jesee Bagget	1
No.	1
Whites	
Thos. Jackson Senr.	1
No.	1
Whites	
Noah Mercer	1
No.	1
Whites	
Hector McNeill	1
Black	2
A Negroe fellow Jack & a wench Nany	
No.	3

Whites	
Duncan Campble & sons Archd. & Hugh & Archd. McKearn [?]ah	4
Black	1
Negro fellow Cuba	
No.	5
Whites	
Joseph Fort & William Hubard	2
Black	5
Negroe fellows Jacob & hary & Wenches Judy: Moll & Patt	
No.	7
Whites	
James Ard	1
Black	3
Negroe fellow simon & wenches Nan & Judy	
No.	4
Whites	
John Mcpharson & Son	2
Black	4
Negroe fellow [Torn] & Negroe Wenches Nany & Bety	
No.	6
Whites	
Daniel Patterson	1
No.	1
Whites	
James McNeill	1
Black	3
Negroe fellows Tony & Tom & a Negroe wench Ka[Torn]	
No.	4
Whites	
Thos. Muzelwhite & sons [Torn] Milbee & [Torn]than	3
No.	3
Whites	
Daniel [Torn] [Torn]	

Whites
[Torn]ee moss [Torn]

Whites
John Boucharty [Torn]

Whites
John Lee & son
Shadrach [Torn] [Torn]

Whites
Henry Bird & sons William
 & Joseph [Torn] [Torn]

Whites
Solomon Johnston Junr.
& wife [Torn] [Torn]

Whites
Joseph Riggen [Torn]
Negroe fellow Quaco two
We[Torn]

Whites
Thomas Jackson Junr. [Torn]

Whites
John Edens [Torn]

Whites
Joseph Bagget & Peter
Lewis [Torn] [Torn]

Whites
John Blunt & son Jacob

Whites
John Blunt Junr. [Torn]

Whites
Phillip Blunt [Torn] [Torn]

Whites
Ralph Riggen   1
No.   1

Whites
John Riggen   1
No.   1

Whites
William Moore & sons James & Matthew   3
No.   3

Whites
John Bullard   1
No.   1

Whites
William moore Junr.   1
No.   1

Whites
Lewis Jenkins   1
No.   1

Whites
Daniel Mudic   1
No.   1

Whites
Samuel Andrews & sons Samuel & absalom 3
No.   3

Cudworth Oxendine [Torn]

Whites
Lewis Hall and son Enoch   2
No.   2

Whites
James Wilkinson   1
No.   1

Whites
Thomas Groome   1
No.   1

Mulatoes   1
[Torn]tterage Lockliar
No.   1

Mulatoes   1
Cannon Cumbo   1
No.   1

Mulatoes   1
Ishmael Chevis   1
No.   1

Whites
Daniel Willis & John Clyburn   2
Black   1
A Negroe fellow Sam
No.   3

Whites
George Willis   1
No.   1

Chapter 2:   Bladen County Tax Lists of 1769

Whites
John Graves ... 1
No. ... 1

Whites
Jesee: Joel: & Thomas
Pittman ... 3
No. ... 3

Whites
Demsy Bairfield ... 1
No. ... 1

Whites
George parson ... 1
No. ... 1

Whites
John Dicks ... 1
No. ... 1

Whites
Thomas Davis ... 1
No. ... 1

Whites
Jacob Silars ... 1
No. ... 1

Whites
Samuel Edwards ... 1
No. ... 1

Mulatoes ... 1
Arthur Lamb
No. ... 1

Whites
Henry Johnston [Torn] ... 1
No. ... 1

Whites
John fiveash [Torn] ... 2
No. ... 2

Whites
Moses Hodge ... 1
No. ... 1

Whites
Daniel McLain ... 1
No. ... 1

Whites
Christopher Garli [Torn] Bairfield ... 2
No. ... 2

Whites
Aaron Odom: Silas [Torn] ... 2
Mulatoes ... 1
John Sweat
No. ... 3

Mulatoes ... 2
Charles & David [Torn]
No. ... 2

Mulatoes ... 1
Simon Cox
No. ... 1

Whites
Samuel Hains ... 1
No. ... 1

Mulatoes ... 2
James Doyal & wife
No. ... 2

Whites
William Ard ... 1
No. ... 1

Whites
John & Edmund Baxsly ... 2
No. ... 2

Whites
Tho. Creal ... 1
No. ... 1

Whites
Jesee muzewhite ... 1
No. ... 1

Whites
William & Ashton [Torn] Baxsly ... 2
No. ... 2

Whites
Mary obodyford & son William & John Fuller ... 2
No. ... 2

Mulatoes ... 1
Peter Cairsey
No. ... 1

Whites
Henry Taylor ... 1
No. ... 1

Whites
[Torn] Whatley   1
No.   1

Mulatoes   1
[Torn] [Torn]mmon
No.   1

Whites
[Torn] [Torn]wter   1
No.   1

Whites
Lazarus Creal   1
No.   1

Mulatoes   2
Richd. Jones & wife
No.   2

Whites
Robert Ferrel   1
Black   1
Negroe wench Grace
No.   2

Whites
Thomas Creal   1
No.   1

Whites
Abram Richardson   1
No.   1

Mulatoes   1
Solomon James Senr.
No.   1

Mulatoes   1
John Wilson
No.   1

Mulatoes   1
Richd. Hammons
No.   1

Whites
Benjamin Odom   1
Mulatoes   1
William Wilkins
No.   2

Whites
Levi & William Sparkman   2
No.   2

Whites
Richd. Sparkman   1
No.   1

Whites
Thos. Cairsey Senr. & son Godfrey & James
Stureyd[Torn]   3
Black   1
Negroe fellow Dick
No.   4

Whites
James Bagget   1
No.   1

Whites
John Ingram & John
D[Torn]ery   2
No.   2

Whites
Thos Ivey   1
Black   1
Obed[Torn]
No.   2

Mulatoes   1
John Russel
No.   1

Mulatoes   1
David Braveboy
No.   1

Whites
Thomas Beagla[Torn]   1
No.   1

Whites
Joab Stapleton & William Hail Junr.   2
No.   2

Whites
Isaac Hall   1
No.   1

Whites
Reuben Roberts & Jacob Done   2
No.   2

Whites
Jacob Blackwell   1
No.   1

Whites
Meredith Ellzey   1
No.   1

Mulatoes   2
Daniel Wharton & wife
No.   2

Whites
William Butler   1
No.   1

Whites
John Branch & Manuwell Talton   2
No.   2

Whites
Daniel Smith & Calep Hughwell   2
No.   2

Whites
William Singleton   1
No.   1

Whites
John Rivers   1
No.   1

Whites
Arthur Bairfield   1
No.   1

Whites
Jeremiah Taylor & Sampson Taylor   2
No.   2

Whites
John Roazer   1
[Torn]

Whites
[Torn] Roazer & William   2
[Torn]

Whites
Thos. Low   1
[Torn]

Whites
Green bodyford   1
[Torn]

Whites
Joseph Strickland   1
No.   1

Whites
Thomas Moore   1
No.   1

Whites
James Stewart   1
No.   1

Mulatoes   1
Thomas Sweat
No.   1

Mulatoes   3
Solomon Johnston & wife & Jacob Braveboy
No.   3

Whites
William Jones   1
No.   1

Whites
William moore Bluf   1
No.   1

Mulatoes   2
James Lowry & William Jones
Black   1
Negroe fellow Jack
No.   3

Whites
John McLaine   1
Mulatoes   4
Joshua perkins & wife & Sons George & Isaac
No.   5

****

BLADEN COUNTY TAX LIST OF 1769

A List of Taxables for the Year 1769   Ralph Miller

Headings for this list include: Whites, Negro Men, Negro Women, Negro Boys, Carriage Wheels, & All.

Jno Poynter & Richard Mullington
Whites   2
Negro Men   2
Negro Women   1
All   5

17

Wm: Bartram
Whites	5
Negro Men	6
Negro Women	4
Negro Boys	1
All	16

John Lucas
Whites	3
Negro Men	7
Negro Women	5
Negro Boys	1
All	16

Donl. McKeithan
Whites	2
Negro Men	1
Negro Women	1
All	4

Jno. Boyd
Whites	1
Negro Women	1
All	2

Dunkn. McKeithan
Whites	1
Negro Men	1
All	2

John Pemberton
Whites	1
Negro Women	1
All	2

Ann Maultby
Whites	2
Negro Men	1
Negro Women	2
All	5

Saml. McRee
Whites	1
Negro Men	3
All	4

Mrs: Waddle
Negro Men	18
Negro Women	16
Negro Boys	1
Carriage Wheels	2
All	35

Moses Homes
Whites	1
Negro Men	1
All	2

Arch: Darrah
Whites	1
Negro Men	1
All	2

Neal Shaw
Whites	2
Negro Men	1
Negro Women	1
All	4

Richd. Singletary
Whites	3
Negro Men	4
Negro Women	1
All	8

Iver McKey
Whites	1
Negro Men	3
Negro Women	2
All	6

James Stewart
Whites	1
Negro Men	1
All	2

Wm. Smith & his son
Whites	2
Negro Men	2
All	4

Jno. Jones Senr. & Junior
Whites	2
Negro Women	2
All	4

Tho Hall Esqr. & Stephn: Britton
Whites	2
Negro Men	12
Negro Women	10
Negro Boys	2
Carriage Wheels	2
All	26

List sent P Robt. Johnston
Whites	2
Negro Men	5
Negro Women	3
All	10

Whites

John O'Deer 1

Turner Davis 1

Richd. Small &
John Young 2

Wm. Forister 1

Wm: Davis 1

Thos: Tooles 1

Danl:McCarter 1

John Small 2

Jacob Messick 1

John Shaw 3

Arch: McKeithan 1

Arch: Bakxter 1

Wm: How 1

Arch: McCarter 2

Arch: Shaw 1

Jonadab Bass[?] 1

Stephen White 1

Herbert Taylor 1

****

BLADEN COUNTY TAX LIST OF 1769

A List of Taxables Taken by Thos. Robeson

Headings for this list include: Whites, Fellows, Wenches, Boys, Girls, & Total.

Whites	1
John Anderson	
Total	1

Whites	1
William Anderson	
Total	1

Whites	2
James Bennit	
Total	2

Whites	3
Neil Beard & two sons	
Fellows	1
Total	4

Whites	1
Daniel Beard	
Total	1

Whites	2
Lawrence Byrne & son Thos.	
Total	2

Whites	1
William Brafford	
Total	1

Whites	2
Samuel & Stephen Butler	
Fellows	4
Wenches	1
Total	7

Whites	2
Benjamin Clark South River	
Total	2

Whites	1
Able Corbit	
Total	1

Whites	1
Benjamin Clark	
Fellows	1
Wenches	1

Whites	3
Wm Cain & two sons	
Total	3

John Willm. _____

Whites	4
Joseph Carter & two sons & Josiah Perkins	
Total	4

Whites	2
Thos. Coplin & James Coplin	
Total	2

Whites	1
John Cashwell	
Total	1

Whites	1
Thomas Cashwell	
Total	1

Whites	1
Samuel Cain	
Fellows	1
Total	2

Whites	1
John Elwell	
Fellows	1
Wenches	1
Total	3

Whites	1
William Edge	
Total	1

Whites	1
Robert Edwards	
Wenches	1
Total	2

Whites	2
John Faris & William Morgan	
Total	2

Whites	2
William Faris & George Stroud	
Total	2

Whites	1
Andrew Graham	
Total	1

Whites	1
William Head	
Total	1

Whites	2
John Hollingsworth	
Total	2

Whites	2
Stephen Hollingsworth & Arthur Spears	
Total	2

Whites	3
Martha Higgins & Wm. McMaster & Jere. Plummer & Thos. Wilkison	
Fellows	1
Total	4

Whites	1
William Johnston	
Total	1

Whites	1
John Jarvis	
Total	1

Whites	2
John Johnston & wife	
Total	2

Whites	1
Ezeciah Jones	
Total	1

Whites	3
John Lock & son & Thos. Chance	
Fellows	1
Wenches	2
Boys	1
Total	7

Whites	1
Ebenezer Low	
Total	1

Whites	1
James McDonald	
Fellows	2
Wenches	3
Total	6

Whites	1
Alexr. McDonald	
Total	1

Whites	2
Archibald & David McDonald	
Total	2

Whites	1
John McDonald	
Total	1

Whites	1
Mathias Monce	
Total	1

Whites	2
Ellephe Plummer & two Sons Wm. & John	
Total	2

Whites	1
John Rogerson	
Total	1

Whites	1
John Richardson Junr.	
Total	

Whites	1
Joseph Ray	
Total	1

Whites	2
Nathaniel Reaves	
Wenches	1
Total	3

Whites	2
Isaac Ray & Wm. McMaster Senr.	
Fellows	2
Wenches	3
Total	7

Whites	1
Thomas Richardson	
Total	1

Whites	1
John Smith South River	
Total	1

Whites	2
Samuel Salton & David Fountin	
Total	2

Whites	1
John Suggs	
Total	1

Whites	2
Thomas Sessoms & son	
Total	2

Whites	4
Benjamin Singletary & two sons Richard, Benjamin & James Singletary	
Fellows	3
Wenches	2
Total	9

Whites	1
Philip Wood	
Total	1

Whites	3
James West & son James & Thos. Bedsole	
Total	3

CHAPTER 3

BLADEN COUNTY TAX LISTS OF 1770

BLADEN COUNTY TAX LIST OF 1770

John Smith Esqr. List ofTaxables for the Year 1770

Headings in this list include: Whites, Molatoes, Black Males, Black Females, & Total.

Whites	
James Benson	1
Total	1

Whites	
Peter Broadus	1
Black Males	1
Black Females	1
Total	3

Whites	
Hezekiah Davis & Lewes Han[Faded]	2
Black Females	1
Total	3

Whites	
Bumbery Day Esqr., Saml Bailey, Saml. Jones & John Munson	4
Black Males	4
Black Females	1
Total	9

Whites	
Benja. Fitzrandolph	1
Black Females	2
Total	3

Whites	
Mathew Gowen[?]	1
Total	1

Whites	
Richd. Huffan	1
Total	1

Whites	
Bray Hargrove & [?]	2
Total	2

Whites	
Hudle Huffam	1
Total	1

Whites	
David & Richard Loyd & Jno. Thomas	3
Black Males	1
Black Females	2
Total	6

Whites	
Francis Lucas	1
Black Males	2
Black Females	2
Total	6

Whites	
David Lock	1
Black Males	2
Black Females	1
Total	4

Whites	
Joseph Lock	1
Black Males	2
Total	3

Whites	
Alexander Mims, Overseer	1
Black Males	1
Black Females	4
Total	6

Whites	
Ephram Mulford	1
Black Males	1
Black Females	2
Total	4

Whites
William Nicloson
Constable
Black Males 1
Total 1

Whites
John Oliphant 1
Total 1

Whites
Joseph Powers 1
Total 1

Whites
John & Jas. Parker 2
Total 2

Whites
Thos. & Eleazer Russ 2
Total 2

Whites
John Russ & [?] Dowey 2
Black Males 1
Total 3

Whites
John Smith 1
Total 1

Whites
John Smith Junr. 1
Black Males 1
Total 2

Whites
John Singletary 1
Black Males 1
Total 2

Whites
Solomon Sanderson 1
Total 1

Whites
Wm., John & James Salter 3
Black Males 4
Black Females 4
Total 11

Whites
Jenet Thomas & son Geo: 1
Total 1

Whites
Geo: & David Thomas & Jno. Drummon 3
Black Males 1
Total 4

Whites
Wm & Mathias [Faded]essel 2
Total 2

Whites
Wm & James Wooley 2
Total 2

Whites
Josiah Wilson & Wm
Shutey 2
Black Males 1
Total 3

****

BLADEN COUNTY TAX LIST OF 1770

Bumbery Day Esqr. List of Taxables for the Year 1770

Headings in this list include: Whites, Molatoes, Black Males, Black Females & Total.

Whites
John Anderson Senr. Patroler & son John 1
Black Males 3
Black Females 1
Total 5

Whites
Stephen Anderson & Jacob Wortham 2
Black Males 2
Total 4

Whites
Joseph Anderson 1
Black Females 1
Total 2

Whites
Willm. Boan 1
Total 1

Whites
Wm. Brigs 1
Total 1

Whites
Edmd. & Richd. Crutchfield 2
Total 2

Whites
Wm Crummarty   1
Total   1

Whites
Thos. Cashwell   1
Total   1

Whites
John Cashwell   1
Total   1

George Gibbs Negroes on Black river
Black Males   5
Black Females   3
Total   8

Whites
John & Henry Hilbourne   2
Total   2

Molatoes   4
Isaac, Jno., Eliza., & Hannah Hayes
Total   4

Whites
Wm Howard & Duncan Grant on Charity   1
Black Males   2
Black Females   1
Total   4

Whites
Joseph Howard   1
Black Males   1
Total   2

Whites
Hezekiah Howard   1
Total   1

Whites
John Henessy   1
Total   1

Whites
John & [Torn] Howard   2
Black Males   2
Black Females   1
Total   5

Whites
Thos. & Josiah Howard   2
Total   2

Whites
Daniel Melvin   1
Total   1

Whites
Nathan Meredith   1
Total   1

Whites
Meial Mixon   1
Total   1

Whites
Edwd. Reives   1
Total   1

Whites
Robert Stewart   1
Black Females   1
Total   2

Whites
Matthew Stephens   1
Total   1

Whites
Wm Stewart   1
Black Males   4
Black Females   4
Total   9

Whites
Jacob Sikes   1
Total   1

Whites
John Sutton   1
Total   1

Whites
Bemont, Christopher & Wm Sutton   3
Black Males   1
Total   4

Whites
John Sikes, Michael Toben & John Cummons
                                              3
Total   3

Whites
John, Wm, & Saml. Smith   3
Black Males   6
Black Females   4
Total   13

Whites
Thomas Suggs   1
Total   1

Whites
Thomas Sessham Senr. & Junr.   2
Total   2

Whites
John Suggs   1
Total   1

Whites
Othnial Cons. Alexr. Strachen, Thos. Hill &
Wm Tabet   3
Black Males   2
Black Females   1
Total   6

Whites
John Trowler[?]   1
Total   1

Whites
Saml. & Jacob Webster   2
Total   2

Whites
James West Senr. Constable & Junr. & James
MCClam[?]   2
Total   2

Whites
Joseph Senr., Junr. &Wm Woodcock   3
Total   3

****

BLADEN COUNTY TAX LIST FOR 1770

John Grange Esqr. List of Taxables for the Year 1770

Headings in this list include: Whites, Mulatoes, Black Males, Black Females, & Total.

Whites   3
Charles Benbow
Black Females   1
Total   4

Whites   1
Joseph Clerk[?]
Black Males   6
Black Females   5
Total   12

Whites   3
John Campbell
Black Males   2
Black Females   1
Total   6

Whites   1
Daniel Currey
Total   1

Whites   1
Berringer Moore
Black Males   5
Black Females   4
Total   13

Roger Moore's Estate Given in by Jno. Campbell
Black Males   21
Black Females   18
Total   39

Whites   2
Mr. Guin Thomas one [?] Chair one Do: with 4
Whites
Black Males   17
Black Females   18
Total   40

Whites   1
John Newto[n]
Black Males   6
Black Females   3
Total   10

Whites   1
Stephen Shepherd
Black Males   1
Total   2

Whites   1
William White
Black Males   1
Black Females   1
Total   3

****

Chapter 3:   Bladen County Tax Lists of 1770

BLADEN COUNTY TAX LIST OF 1770

George Brown Esqr List of Taxables 1770

Headings in this list include: White Males, Mulatoes, Black Males, Black Females, & Total.

White Males
Thomas Avery | 1
Total | 1

White Males
Dennis Collom | 1
Total | 1

White Males
Thomas & James Copeland | 2
Total | 2

White Males
Even Ellis & Ephraim Lemmon[?] | 2
Black Males | 1
Black Females | 1
Total | 4

White Males
William Ellis | 1
Total | 1

White Males
Stephen Freeman, Constable | 1
Total | 1

White Males
John Harrison & James Issum | 2
Black Males | 1
Total | 3

White Males
Richard Harrison | 1
Black Males | 2
Total | 3

White Males
Alexander Harvey | 1
Total | 1

White Males
Isaach Jones & son Edward | 2
Black Males | 3
Black Females | 2
Total | 7

White Males
Joseph Kamp | 1
Black Females | 1
Total | 2

White Males
Robert McRee | 1
Total | 1

White Males
William Owens | 1
Black Males | 2
Total | 3

White Males
Thomas [Torn] | 1
Total | 1

White Males
Griffeth Jones White | 1
Black Males | 2
Total | 3

White Males
John Senr., David & Matthew White | 3
Black Males | 1
Black Females | 2
Total | 6

White Males
William White | 1
Black Males | 1
Total | 2

White Males
John White Junr | 1
Black Males | 1
Total | 2

Black Males | 1
Black Females | 1
Moses Walker & wife
Free Negroes
Total | 2

White Males
Richard Salter | 1
Black Males | 1
Black Females | 1
Total | 3

White Males
John Yats | 1
Total | 1

****

BLADEN COUNTY TAX LIST OF 1770

A List of the Taxable Property of the Inhabitants of Samuel Cains Company, May 30th 1770

Property value in this list is given in English Pounds.

Archibald Little
£75-1-4

Neil Thomson
£85-8

Donald McTigret
£50

Wm McMullin
£103-4

Macom McMillan
£74-4

Wm Bleu
£82-1

Arthor Barfil
£1-14-2

Levy Glass
£754-6

Solomon Glass
£40-8

Thos Kervin
£34-[Torn]

John Carter
£4-[Torn]

Charles Counsil
£78-[Torn]

Absalom Legett
£103 [Torn]

Benja. Britt
£96 [Torn]

Uriah Lamberson
£42 [Torn]

Wm McDonald
£42 [Torn]

Judith Corbett
£110 [Torn]

John Johnson
£58-8

Duncan Buey
£91
Total £1956-1-4

Daniel McEachorn
£221-0 8

Locklor Camron
£67

Archey Belbon
£40-1-2

Benja. Lancaster
£70

Saml. Canada
£544-1

John Sinklor
£14

Archibald McGugan
£87

Donold Mc[?]eel
£110

Mordock McCloud
£30

Daniel Mathus
£11

Wm Taylor
£240-2

Donald McNeil
Total £1502-4-10

Jeremiah Willis
£22

David Young
£116-6-10

Daniel Patison
£170-15

Andrew Puff[?]
£180

David Legett
£41-5

Lewis Munrow
£206

John Bohodd
£249

Philip Ikener
£178

James Ard
£161

John McCollom
£49

Neil McCalpin
£18-10

Alx. Little
£26-9

Jas. McNeil
£1036

Jas. Biggs
£60-6

John Gattes[?]
£[Torn]-4

Joseph Corbett
£86-6

Macom McNear
£32-4

Total £2634
Assesors

	Pole Tax
John Ward	
Wm Herring	£103-60
Henry Mercer	£691-8
Total Sum	£8304-17

****

BLADEN COUNTY TAX LIST OF 1770

Peter Lord Esqr. List of Taxables for the Year 1770

Headings in this list include: Whites, Mulatoes, Black Males, Black Females, & Total.

Whites	
John Ansly	1
Total	1
Whites	
Oxford Beasley	1
Total	1
Whites	
Samuel Beltman	1
Total	1
Whites	
John Bohard	1
Mulatoes	1
Total	2
Whites	
Briton Barnes	1
Total	1
Whites	
Simon Bundey	1
Black Males	3
Black Females	2
Total	6
Whites	
John Barrey	1
Total	1
Whites	
Absalom Collans	1
Total	1
Whites	
Abel Corbit	1
Total	1
Whites	
Joseph & Benjamin Cooper	2
Black Males	2
Total	4
Whites	
Bunkley & Joseph Corbit	2
Total	2

Chapter 3: Bladen County Tax Lists of 1770

Whites
Samuel & Jacob Canneday 2
Black Males 1
Black Females 1
Total 4

Whites
Samuel Canneday Junr. 1
Total 1

Whites
Isaac Canneday & Archa. Boon 2
Black Males 1
Total 3

Whites
John Crees 1
Total 1

Mulatoes 1
John Combow
Total 1

Whites
James Ellis, Thos. Moore & John Blank 3
Black Males 2
Black Females 2
Total 7

Whites
Richd. Elwell 1
Total 1

Whites
Andrew Gunderson, Captain Johnstons Overseer 1
Black Males 2
Black Females 1
Total 4

Whites
Levy Glass 1
Mulatoes 1
Black Females 2
Total 4

Whites
Jesse Glass & Uriah Lamberson 2
Total 2

Whites
Michael Husters 1
Total 1

Whites
Abel Holton 1
Total 1

Whites
George Ikener 1
Mulatoes 1
Total 2

Whites
Phillip Ikner & son Mical 2
Total 2

Whites
James Jackson 1
Total 1

Whites
William Kirkpatrick, Thos. Armatage & Jno. Pettenger 3
Black Males 1
Black Females 1
Total 5

Whites
Lenord Lock 1
Black Males 1
Black Females 1
Total 3

Whites
John Lock & Thomas Chance 2
Black Males 2
Black Females 2
Total 6

Whites
Archabald Little 1
Total 1

Whites
John Legett & Richard Wilkinson 2
Total 2

Whites
John Moore 1
Total 1

Whites
Willm Moore & son Matthew 2
Total 2

Whites
Willm. Moore Junr. 1
Total 1

Whites
John Mason   1
Total   1

Whites
Henry Messer   1
Black Males   1
Total   2

Whites
Hector McNeal   1
Black Males   1
Black Females   1
Total   3

Whites
James McNeal   1
Black Males   2
Black Females   1
Total   4

Whites
Neal McNeal   1
Total   1

Whites
Danel McDuffee   1
Total   1

Whites
James Moore   1
Total   1

Whites
Wm. Maultsby & Brother   2
Total   2

Whites
James Moon   1
Total   1

Whites
Wm. McMarrick   1
Total   1

Whites
Joseph Mott   1
Total   1

Whites
Jesse Newbery & Jno. Harvey   2
Black Males   4
Black Females   1
Total   7

Whites
John Newbery Junr.   1
Black Males   2
Black Females   1
Total   4

Whites
John Newbery Senr.   1
Black Males   1
Black Females   1
Total   3

Whites
Isaiah Powell   1
Total   1

Whites
Andrew Pusley   1
Total   1

Whites
Daniel Peterson   1
Total   1

Whites
Joseph Price & son John   2
Total   2

Whites
John Storm   1
Total   1

Whites
Benjamin Sims & Joseph
Hogs   2
Total   2

Whites
John Stanton   1
Black Females   1
Total   2

Whites
James Sims Senr. & sons Isaac & Robert &
Coson James   4
Black Females   1
Total   5

Whites
Tobias Sealey   1
Total   1

Whites
James Sims Junr.   1
Total   1

Whites
Joseph Thims & son Jesse 2
Total 2

Whites
Robert Upton 1
Total 1

Whites
Richard Upton 1
Total 1

Whites
Agerton Willis & Benja. & son Benja., Jas. Blair
& Jno McMoth 5
Black Males 18
Black Females 7
Total 30

Whites
Edmison Weer 1
Black Males 6
Black Females 3
Total 10

Whites
David Young 1
Total 1

****

BLADEN COUNTY TAX LIST OF 1770

Thomas Robeson Junr. List of Taxables for the Year 1770

Headings in this list include: Whites Mulatoes, Black Males, Black Females, & Total

Whites
Wm Anderson 1
Total 1

Whites
John Anderson 1
Total 1

Whites
Laurance Byrne & 3 sons 4
Total 4

Whites
Neill Beard & son James 2
Black Males 1
Total 3

Whites
Wm. Bruford 1
Total 1

Whites
Joseph Birkett & sons Joseph & Joh[n] ... 3
Total 3

Whites
Daniel Beard 1
Total 1

Whites
Samuel & Stephen Butler 2
Black Males 4
Black Females 1
Total 7

Whites
James Bennet 1
Total

Whites
Joseph Carter & son Henry 2
Total 2

Whites
Wm Caine & sons John & Willm. 3
Total 3

Whites
Benja. Clark & son Henry 2
Total 2

Whites
Benja. Clark 1
Black Male 1
Black Female 1
Total 3

Whites
Samuel Cain [Cairn?] 1
Black Males 1
Total 2

Whites
Robert Edward & John Beard 2
Black Males 2
Total 4

Whites
John Ferris & William Morgan 2
Total 2

Whites	
Wm Ferris & Jas. Thomas	2
Black Males	1
Black Females	1

Whites	
Robert Grice	1
Total	1

Whites	
Andrew Grimes & Archa. McDonald	2
Total	2

Whites	
Martha Higgens & Wm. McMaster	1
Black Males	1

Whites	
Stephen Hallingsworth & Son Isaac	2
Total	2

Whites	
John Hollingsworth	1
Total	1

Whites	
Merede Honeycut	1
Total	1

Whites	
Isaac Jessup	1
Total	1

Mulatoes	2
John Johnston & Wife	
Total	2

Whites	
John Jervis	1
Total	1

Whites	
Wm. Johnston & son James	2
Total	2

Whites	
Thomas Lock	1
Total	1

Whites	
Matthew Muns	1
Total	1

Whites	
Wm McMaster Junr.	1
Total	1

Whites	
James & David McDonald	2
Black Males	2
Black Females	1
Total	5

Whites	
John McDonald	1
Black Females	1
Total	2

Whites	
Wm. McRee	1
Black Males	7
Black Females	2
Total	10

Mulatoes	2
Titus Overton & Wife	
Total	2

Whites	
Jeremiah Plummer	1
Total	1

Whites	
Elephey Plummer & two sons Wm & John	2
Total	2

Whites	
Joseph Ray	1
Total	1

Whites	
John Richardson & Saml. Carver	2
Total	2

Whites	
Robert Richardson	1
Total	1

Whites	
[?] [?]	1
Black Males	2
Black Females	3
Total	6

Whites	
Nathaniel & Darten Reeves	2
Black Females	1
Total	3

Whites
James Singletary & Peter Carpenter   2
Black Male   1
Total   3

Whites
Benja. Singletary & 2 sons Benja. & Jas.   3
Black Males   2
Black Females   2
Total   7

Whites
Richd. Singletary   1
Total   1

Whites
Jacob Storgenor   1
Black Males   3
Black Females   1
Total   5

Whites
Samuel Sutton & Josiah Johnston   2
Total   2

Whites
George Stroud   1
Total   1

Whites
John Smith & Richard Hammons   2
Total   2

****

BLADEN COUNTY TAX LIST OF 1770

Abram Barnes[?] Esqrs List of Taxables for the Year 1770

Headings for this list include: Whites, Molatoes, Black Males, Black Females, & Total.

Whites
William Brumbell   1
Total   1

Whites
Charles Bullock   1
Total   1

Whites
Edmund Brown   1
Total   1

Whites
Thomas Brown Senr. & Thos. Brown & Richd.
King   3
Total   3

Whites
Dempsey Barefield   1
Total   1

Whites
Charles Barefield   1
Total   1

Whites
Rodger Barefield   1
Total   1

Whites
John Barnes   1
Total   1

Whites
William Baker   1
Total   1

Whites
Benja., Nathan & Jesse Britt   3
Total   3

Molatoes   2
John Bullard & Gutridge Lockelier
Total   2

Whites
David Bairfield   1
Molatoes   1
Benja. Lamby[?]
Total   2

Whites
John, Britton Branch & Edmund Falton [Fulton]
   3
Total   3

Whites
Shadrach Bagget & Joseph Strickland   2
Total   2

Whites
William Coward   1
Total   1

Molatoes   1
Simon Cox
Total   1

Chapter 3:   Bladen County Tax Lists of 1770

Molatoes	2
Gilbert Cox & James Percey	
Total	2

Molatoes	1
Cannon Cumbo	
Total	1

Whites	
Thomas Cross	1
Total	1

Molatoes	3
James Carter Senr. & Junr.& Isaac Carter	
Total	3

Whites	
George & Matthew Colson	2
Total	2

Whites	
Bedreddon Caraway & Josiah Taylor	2
Total	2

Whites	
George Calley & Josiah Harp [Hasp]	2
Total	2

Whites	
Thomas Davis	1
Total	1

Whites	
Richard Folk	1
Total	1

Whites	
Edmund & John Flowers & Willm Barret	3
Total	3

Whites	
Ignatious Flowers	1
Total	1

Whites	
John & Dempsey Fiveash	2
Total	2

Whites	
Joseph Fort & Michael Barnes	2
Black Males	2
Black Females	3
Total	7

Whites	
Stephen Gleer	1
Black Females	1
Total	2

Whites	
James Granthan	1
Total	1

Whites	
William Granthan	1
Total	1

Whites	
Richard Granthan	1
Total	1

Molatoes	2
Frederick Goan & Wife	
Total	2

Whites	
John Hutson	1
Molatoes	1
John Waldon	
Total	2

Whites	
Nathan Horn	1
Total	1

Whites	
James Inman & Henry Howser[?]	2
Total	2

Molatoes	1
Adam Ivey	
Total	1

Whites	
Benja. Ivey	1
Molatoes	1
John Phillips	
Total	2

Whites	
Hardey Inman	1
Total	1

Whites	
William Jones	1
Total	1

Whites	
Thomas Low	1
Total	1

Whites
Shadrach Huit   1
Molatoes   2
Isaac & Needhan Lamb
Total   3

Molatoes   1
Arthur Lamb
Total   1

Whites
Thomas Moore, Thos. Bennet Simon Trent,
Henry Deberrey   4
Total   4

Whites
Archabald McKissak   1
Black Males   2
Black Females   1
Total   4

Whites
Thomas Odom & Barnabas Lamb   2
Black Males   1
Total   3

Whites
John, Wm & Aron Odom   3
Total   3

Whites
Benja. Odom & Wm Smith   2
Molatoes   1
Wm Wilkins
Total   3

Whites
Caraway Oats   1
Total   1

Molatoes   1
Charles Oxendine
Total   1

Whites
Sarah Oxendine & Willm Taner   1
Total   1

Whites
George Parsons   1
Total   1

Whites
Joseph, John & Willm. Phillips   3
Total   3

Whites
Thomas Pitman   1
Total   1

Whites
Jesse Pitman   1
Total   1

Whites
Thomas Procter   1
Total   1

Whites
Joseph Pines[?]   1
Total   1

Whites
Joel Pitman Constable   0
Total   0

Whites
Thomas & James Rowland   2
Total   2

Whites
Richard Sparkman   1
Total   1

Molatoes   1
Elisha Sweeting
Total   1

Whites
John & Jesse Smith   2
Black Males   8
Black Females   3
Total   13

Whites
[?] Sparkman   1
Total   1

Molatoes   1
Sarah & James Sweet
Total   1

Whites
Charles & Wm Thompson   2
Total   2

Whites
Jonathan Taylor   1
Total   1

Whites
James Trowell   1
Total   1

Whites
Samuel & Thomas Troler [Tyler?]   2
Total   2

Whites
Cornelias & William Terrel   2
Total   2

Whites
John Turner   1
Black Males   5
Black Females   4
Total   10

Whites
George Willis   1
Total   1

Whites
Daniel Willis, Jno. Claybon & Lark[?] Thomas
                                                              3
Black Male   1
Total   4

Whites
David Williams   1
Total   1

Molatoes   2
Daniel Wharton & Wife
Total   2

Whites
Isaac Wilks   1
Total   1

****

BLADEN COUNTY TAX LIST OF 1770

William McRee Esqr. List of Taxables for the Year 1770

Headings for this list include: Whites, Molatoes, Black Males, Black Females & Total.

Whites
George, Thomas & John Brown   3
Black Males   2
Black Females   2
Total   7

Whites
James Bailey & Neill McDuffee   2
Black Males   7
Black Females   2
Total   11

Whites
Edwd. & David Bryan   2
Black Males   1
Total   3

Whites
Amey Bryan   0
Black Males   1
Black Females   1
Total   2

Whites
John Bentley   1
Total   1

Whites
John Bryan & William Dowlas   2
Black Females   1
Total   3

Whites
Philoman Bryan   1
Black Females   1
Total   2

Whites
Robert Baker   1
Black Males   1
Total   2

Whites
Henry Bosswell   1
Total   1

Whites
Margaret Byrne
Black Males   5
Black Females   3
Total   8

Whites
John Berrey   1
Total   1

Whites	
Maturin Colvill	1
Black Males	1
Black Females	1
Total	3

Whites	
Alexander Chapman	1
Black Males	4
Total	5

Whites	
Samuel Currey	1
Total	1

Whites	
Richard Chesher	1
Total	1

Whites	
Wm, John & James Caine	3
Black Males	4
Black Females	1
Total	8

Whites	
Joseph Caine	1
Black Males	1
Black Females	1
Total	3

Whites	
Hezekiah, Ephraim Doane & Samuel Brazwell	3
Black Males	6
Black Females	4
Total	13

Whites	
Edward Davis & Frances Owen	2
Black Females	1
Total	3

Whites	
John Dryden	1
Total	1

Whites	
John Denis[?]	1
Total	1

Whites	
Samuel Gayton	1
Total	1

Whites	
Benjamin Humphreys	1
Total	1

Whites	
Thomas, Wm. & John Hestus	3
Total	3

Whites	
Stephen Hestus	1
Total	1

Whites	
John Hill	1
Total	1

Whites	
Josiah Handen Senr. & James Bridges	2
Black Males	2
Total	4

Whites	
Josiah Handen Junr. & Phillip Powell Mattock	2
Black Males	2
Black Females	1
Total	5

Whites	
Wm [Faded]	1
Black Males	1
Black Females	1
Total	3

Whites	
Elizabeth Harrison & sons John & Edward	2
Black Males	2
Black Females	1
Total	5

Whites	
John King	1
Total	1

Whites	
Thomas Kinlaw	1
Total	1

Whites	
Peter Lord	1
Black Males	5
Black Females	3
Total	9

Chapter 3: Bladen County Tax Lists of 1770

Whites
Dennis & John Lennon & Melekiah Messer 3
Black Males 3
Black Females 1
Total 7

Whites
Robert McConkey 1
Black Males 1
Black Females 1
Total 3

Whites
John McGlachlen 1
Total 1

Whites
John Morgan 1
Total 1

Whites
Jonthn & James Moorehead 2
Black Males 2
Total 4

Whites
Jacob Mons 1
Total 1

Whites
Angus McKay 1
Total 1

Whites
Daniel McKeithan 1
Black Males 1
Black Females 1
Total 3

Whites
David Mosley [Morley?] 1
Black Males 2
Black Females 1
Total 4

Whites
John Oviter[?] & Wm. Blocker 2
Total 2

Whites
John Owens & Owens [?]sadey 2
Black Males 8
Black Females 2
Total 12

Whites
Thomas & Scott Owens[?] 2
Black Males 12
Black Females 7
Total 21

Whites
[Faded] [Faded] 3
Total 3

Whites
Thomas Robeson Senr. & Perter[?] 2
Black Males 6
Black Females 6
Total 14

Whites
John Russ Junr. & son 2
Total 2

Whites
David Russ 1
Total 1

Whites
Thomas Robeson Junr. 1
Black Males 3
Black Females 2
Total 6

Whites
James Richardson, Jno Rodgers, & Jas.
Fairecloath 3
Black Males 6
Black Females 4
Total 13

Whites
Wm & Edmd Russ 2
Total 2

Whites
Joseph Singletary & Wm Singletary 2
Black Males 1
Black Females 1
Total 4

Whites
Wm Singletary & Frances Maus 2
Black Males 1
Black Females 1
Total 4

Whites
Thomas Simpson   1
Black Females   2
Total   3

Whites
John & Thomas Screven[?]   2
Total   2

Whites
John Storm   1
Total   1

Whites
Benja. & Richd. Thomas   2
Total   2

Whites
Lewis Thomas   1
Total   1

Whites
David White, James Irvin, & John Porter   3
Molatoes   3
Total   6

Whites
Wm Wilkinson   1
Total   1

Whites
Joseph Wood & Anthony Fisher[?]   2
Total   2

Whites
James Wilson   1
Total   1

Whites
Levey Young   1
Black Males   1
Black Females   2
Total   4

Whites
John & Peter Yates   2
Total   2

****

BLADEN COUNTY TAX LIST OF 1770

John Turner Esqr. List of Taxables for the Year 1770

Headings in this list include: Whites, Mulatoes, Black Males, Black Females & Total.

Whites
Stephen Bryan   1
Total   1

Whites
George Bruer[?]   1
Total   1

Whites
William Burney   1
Black Males   2
Black Females   2
Total   5

Whites
William Burney   1
Total   1

Whites
James Baldwin   1
Black Males   1
Black Females   1
Total   3

Whites
Morris Biven & Thos. Jones   2
Total   2

Whites
John & Charles Baldwin   2
Black Males   3
Black Females   2
Total   7

Whites
Nathaniel Busby   1
Total   1

Whites
Jeremiah Bigford Senr. & Junr. & Willm.   3
Black Females   1
Total   4

Whites
Thomas Bryan   1
Total   1

Whites
Simon & Buho[?] Brite   2
Total   2

Whites	
Simon Burney	1
Total	1

Whites	
William Bryan	1
Black Males	1
Black Females	1
Total	3

Whites	
William Barefoot	1
Black Males	1
Total	2

Whites	
Benjamin Busby	1
Total	1

Whites	
Thomas Childs Overseer to Eagles Estate	1
Black Males	18
Black Females	17
Total	36

Whites	
John Cook	1
Total	1

Whites	
John Conelly	1
Total	1

Whites	
John Cohoon	1
Total	1

Whites	
John Cohoon	1
Total	1

Whites	
James Cohoon	1
Total	1

Whites	
Micajah Cohoon	1
Total	1

Whites	
James Clardy & Wm. Standfast	2
Black Males	1
Total	3

Whites	
John Campbell	1
Total	1

Whites	
John & Zacha. Chancey	2
Total	2

Whites	
James Dupree, Richd., Boyd, & Robt Cohorn	3
Black Males	1
Black Females	1
Total	4

Whites	
John Ellis, Wm & Jas. Ellis & Robert	4
Black Males	3
Black Females	1
Total	8

Whites	
John Etheridge	1
Total	1

Whites	
Saml. & Marmaduke Etheridge	2
Black Males	1
Black Females	1
Total	4

Whites	
John Ellis Junr.	1
Total	1

Black Females	2
Susannah & Rachael Freeman	
Total	2

Whites	
John, James & Jacob Folks	3
Total	3

Black Males	3
Abram, Saml, & Rodger Freeman	
Total	3

Whites	
[Torn] Gibs	1
Black Males	3
Black Females	3
Total	7

Whites	
John Gibbs	1
Black Males	7
Black Females	7
Total	15

Whites	
Isaac Green	1
Black Males	8
Black Females	2
Total	11

Whites	
John Green & James Gifferd	2
Black Males	1
Total	3

Whites	
James Green	1
Black Males	1
Black Females	2
Total	4

Whites	
Abram Gray	1
Total	1

Whites	
John Green	1
Black Males	1
Black Females	2
Total	4

Whites	
John, Willm & Simon Green	3
Black Males	3
Black Females	1
Total	7

Whites	
William Green	1
Total	1

Whites	
David Howell & George Raybon	2
Total	2

Whites	
Saml., John & Malekiah Hughs	3
Total	3

Whites	
Joshua Hays Constable	1
Black Males	1
Total	2

Whites	
John Hilliard Senr. & son John	2
Total	2

Whites	
Mathew Kelly & John Bartaris[?]	2
Black Males	2
Black Females	2
Total	6

Whites	
Frances Lawson & William Register	2
Total	2

Whites	
James & Solomon Lewis	2
Total	2

Whites	
Josiah Lewis Senr. & Son Josiah	2
Black Males	1
Total	3

Whites	
Hanson Lewis & Josiah Lewis	2
Black Males	1
Black Females	1
Total	4

Whites	
Jesse Lankester & Ralph Bowman	2
Total	2

Whites	
Benja. & Richd. Lambethson	2
Black Males	2
Black Females	4
Total	8

Whites	
James Lovet	1
Black Males	1
Black Females	2
Total	4

Whites	
Darbey Murphey & John McLarin	2
Total	2

Whites	
Willm McNeill & David Bailey	2
Black Males	3
Black Females	2
Total	7

Chapter 3: Bladen County Tax Lists of 1770

Whites
Neill McCoulsky, Neil Schaw & Charles
McNorton   3
Black Males   1
Black Females   1
Total   4

Whites
Mathew Moore & Richd. Raynolds   2
Black Males   2
Black Females   2
Total   6

Whites
John McColskey   1
Black Males   1
Total   2

Whites
James Murphey   1
Total   1

Whites
Thomas McClennon   1
Total   1

Whites
John, Robt., Wm. McCowen & Jno McLeron   4
Total   4

Whites
Archabal & James McColeskey   2
Total   2

Whites
Andrew & John McLennon   2
Black Males   1
Black Females   1
Total   4

Whites
Thomas Mims   1
Black Males   1
Total   2

Whites
David Mims   1
Total   1

Whites
Daniel Norton, Jacob & Miles Potter   3
Total   3

Whites
Jacob Norton   1
Total   1

Whites
John Powell Senr. & Abram & John   3
Black Males   2
Black Females   1
Total   6

Whites
Benja. Putnill[?]   1
Total   1

Whites
Charles Raybon   1
Total   1

Whites
John Raybon   1
Total   1

Whites
Richd [Torn]hill   1
Total   1

Whites
Joseph [Torn]er   1
Total   1

Whites
Samuel [Torn]   1
Black Males   2
Total   3

Whites
John & Richard Stubbs   2
Total   2

Whites
Hugh Stewart   1
Total   1

Whites
Peter Simpson   1
Total   1

Whites
Zacariah Smith   1
Black Males   1
Total   2

Whites
Daniel Shipman Senr., Daniel & James   3
Black Males   2
Total   5

Whites
Daniel Schaw   1
Black Males   1
Black Females   1
Total   3

Whites
Alexr. Stewart & John Kelley   2
Black Males   1
Total   3

Whites
John Smith   1
Total   1

Whites
John Simpson   1
Total   1

Whites
Daniel Turner   1
Total   1

Whites
John Tyson   1
Total   1

Whites
John & Isham Wiggans   2
Total   2

Whites
Berry Watts   1
Total   1

Whites
Isaac Wolf   1
Total   1

****

BLADEN COUNTY TAX LIST OF 1770

Archd. McKissak Esqr. List of Taxables for the Year 1770

Headings in this list include: Whites, Mulatoes, Black Males, Black Females & Total.

Whites
William Ard   1
Total   1

Whites
Samuel Andrews Cons. & Sons Saml. &
Absalom   3
Total   3

Whites
James Ard & Three Sons   4
Black Males   1
Black Females   2
Total   7

Whites
Jacob Alford & Jeremiah Gullidge   2
Total   2

Whites
John Blunt & sons Jacob, James & Aron Baxley
                                                4
Black Males   1
Total   5

Whites
Jesse Begget   1
Total   1

Whites
William Baxley   1
Total   1

Whites
John & Edmund Baxley   2
Total   2

Mulatoes   1
David Braveboy
Total   1

Whites
Abram Barnes, Jacob Odom & Wm Wilkinson
                                                3
Black Males   1
Black Females   2
Total   6

Whites
Mary Bodeford & Son Wm.   1
Total   1

Whites
Henry Bird & son Wm.   1
Total   1

Whites
John Bullard   1
Total   1

Whites
Phillip Blunt   1
Total   1

Whites
Joseph Bagget   1
Total   1

Whites
Benja. Britt Junr.   1
Total   1

Whites
Edward Brown   1
Total   1

Whites
Melcom Buy   1
Black Males   1
Total   2

Whites
Elizabeth Best, sons Jno., Archalaus & Bryan   3
Total   3

Whites
Wm Butler   1
Total   1

Whites
Dunkan Campbell & Archa. & Hugh   3
Black Males   1
Total   4

Whites
Thomas Creel   1
Total   1

Whites
Lazarus Creel   1
Total   1

Whites
Thos. Causey Senr.   1
Total   1

Mulatoes   2
Peter Causey & Son David
Total   2

Whites
James Crafts   1
Total   1

Mulatoes   1
Joseph Clark
Total   1

Whites
John Causey & Son   2
Black Males   1
Black Females   1
Total   4

Mulatoes   1
Ishmael Cheeves
Total   1

Whites
[Torn]mas Cau[Torn]
Junr.   1
Total   1

Whites
Elisha, George & Joseph Downing   3
Total   3

Whites
John Dunbar   1
Total   1

Whites
Benja. Dees   1
Total   1

Whites
John Dunkan   1
Total   1

Mulatoes   2
James Doyel & Wife
Total   2

Whites
John Edens   1
Total   1

Whites
Samuel Edwards   1
Total   1

Whites
Benja. Fuller   1
Black Males   1
Total   2

Whites
Wm & Dempsey Fuller   2
Total   2

Whites	
William Truman	1
Total	1

Whites	
Wm Gooden & Son Wm.	2
Total	2

Whites	
Moses & Robert Grice	2
Total	2

Mulatoes	1
Thos. Groom	
Total	1

Whites	
Wm. Gulledge	1
Total	1

Whites	
Chambers Humphry	1
Total	1

Whites	
Jesse Harrol	1
Black Males	1
Total	2

John Hammons	1
Mulatoes	1
Total	1

Whites	
Samuel Hains & Wm Smith	2
Total	2

Whites	
Moses Hodge	1
Mulatoes	1
Jacob Braveboy	
Total	2

Whites	
Lewis & Isaac Hall	2
Total	2

Whites	
Enuch Hall	1
Total	1

Whites	
Thomas & John Jackson	2
Total	2

Mulatoes	2
Richd. Jones & Wife	
Total	2

Whites	
Thomas Ivey	1
Total	1

Whites	
English Thomas Jackson	1
Total	1

Whites	
Lewis Jorkens[?]	1
Total	1

Mulatoes	1
Solomon James	
Total	1

Mulatoes	2
Solomon Johnston & Wife	
Total	2

Mulatoes	2
Solomon Johnston Junr. & Wife	
Total	2

Whites	
James Ivey	1
Total	1

Whites	
Joseph Ivey	1
Total	1

Mulatoes	1
Majour Locklier	
Total	1

Whites	
Peter Lewis	1
Total	1

Whites	
John & Shadrach Lee	2
Total	2

Mulatoes	2
James Lowry & Wm Jones	
Black Males	1
Total	3

Whites	
Thomas Little	1
Total	1

Mulatoes   1
Jacob Lockleer
Total   1

Mulatoes   3
John Lockleer & Wife & son Wm.
Total   3

Whites
John & Daniel [Torn]on   2
Black Males   2
Black Females   2
Total   6

Whites
Peter & Neill [Torn]et   2
Total   2

Whites
Turkell & Lachlen [Torn]ill
& Gilbert McN[Torn]

Joseph [Torn]es
The Rest of the above tax list is missing.

****

BLADEN COUNTY TAX LIST OF 1770

A List of Taxes from Carvers Creek to BrownsCreek taken by Joseph Clark Esqr. and returnable to August Court 1770

Headings for this list include: Master or Mistresses Names, White Men, Negroe Men Slaves, Female Slaves, Boys under Sixteen years, & Total.

Master   John Jones
White Men: John Jones
Female Slaves: Bella & Judith
Boys Under Sixteen: Simon & Present
Total   5

Master   Jacob Meswick
White Men: Jacob Meswick
Total   1

Master   John Lucas
White Men: John Lucas, Jesse Oliphant, & James Carver
Negroe Men Slaves: Will, Johny, Piner, Boger, Dusk, Cezar
Female Slaves: Sue, Lettis, Moll, Lucy, Kate
Boys Under Sixteen: Peter & Will
Total   16

Master   Ralph Miller
White Men: Ralph Miller Junr. & James Morrison
Negroe Men Slaves: York & Seter
Female Slaves: Flora, Jude & Penny
Boys Under Sixteen: Jamie
Total   9

Master   Richd. Singletary
White Men: Richd. Singletary, Benj. Singletary, William Singletary
Negroe Men Slaves: Pompey, Charles & Thomas
Female Slaves: Lucy
Boys Under Sixteen: Pompey
Total   8

Master   William Forester
White Men: William Forester
Total   1

Master   William Davis
White Men: William Davis
Total   1

Master   Daniel McFatter
White Men: Daniel McFatter, Archibald McFatter
Total   2

Master   John Pointer
White Men: John Pointer, Richd. Mullington, & John Pointer Junr.
Negroe Men Slaves: Caesar & Fortune
Female Slaves: Moll
Total   6

Master   Moses Holmes
White Men: Moses Holmes
Total   1

Master   Iver McKoy
White Men: Iver Mckoy
Negroe Men Slaves: Anthony & Prince
Female Slaves: Phillis, Diana & Chloe
Total   6

Master   William Smith
White Men: William Smith & John Smith
Negroe Men Slaves: Will & Prince
Total   4

Chapter 3:   Bladen County Tax Lists of 1770

Master   Neil Schaw
White Men: Neil Schaw, Alexr. Schaw, & Christopher Goodwin
Negroe Men Slaves: Nero & Will
Female Slaves: Doll
Total   6

Master   John O Dear
White Men: John O Dear
Total   1

Master   John Pemberton
White Men: John Pemberton & James Pemberton
Negroe Men Slaves: Dick
Female Slaves: Doll
Total   4

Master Archibald Darroch
White Men: Archbald Darroch, John White, & John Roberts
Negroe Men Slaves: Harry
Total   4

Master   Dougal Blue
White Men: Dougal Blue
Total   1

Master   John Wolf
White Men: John Wolf & Matthew Parker
Total   2

Master   Bryan Green
White Men: Bryan Green & Jno Holland
Total   2

Master   Stephen White
White Men: Stephen White
Total   1

Master   John Boyd
White Men: John Boyd, John Boyd Junr. & Charles Oar[?]
Female Slaves: Minerva
Total   4

Master   Daniel McFatter
White Men: Daniel McFatter
Total   1

Master   William Howe
White Men: William Howe
Total   1

Master   Thomas Jones
White Men: Thomas Jones
Total   1

Master Duncan McKeithan
White Men: Duncan McKeithan
Negroe Men Slaves: Abram
Total   2

Master   Archd. McBride
White Men: Archd. McBride & Malcom McBride
Total   2

Master   Richard Small
White Men: Richard Small & John Young
Total   2

Master   John Schaw
White Men: John Schaw & Malcom Schaw
Total   2

Mistress   Ann Maulsby
White Men: Jas. Maulsby & Saml. Maulsby
Negroe Men Slaves: Scipio
Female Slaves: Jeany, Amber
Total   5

Master   Saml. McKree
White Men: Saml. McKree
Negro Men Slaves: Jamie, Coffee & Quash
Total   4

Master Archbald McKeithan
White Men: Archd. McKeithan
Total   1

Master   John Small
White Men: John Small Const.
Total   [No Taxables]

Master   Jonadab Russ
White Men: Jonadab Russ
Total   1

Master   Benoni Clayton
White Men: Benoni Clayton
Total   1

Master   Archbald Baxter
White Men: Archd. Baxter
Total   1

Master Hugh Waddell Esqr.
White Men: Hugh Waddell Esqr. overseer

Negro Men Slaves:	12
Female Slaves	16
Boys Under Sixteen:	5
Two Wheeled Chairs	1
Total	35

Master John Grainge Esqr.
White Men: John Grainge Esqr., Thos. Grainge, & John Conner
Negroe Men Slaves: Job, Cook, Benny, Jacob, Toney, Jack, Soney, Dinnas, Stepney, Coffee, & Bonny
Female Slaves: Dinah, Kate, Molly, Amy, Comba, Parrina, Bessey, Sara, Grace, Esther, Hanna, Elsey, Hagar, Nanny, Mara, Diana, & Nelly
Boys Under Sixteen: Quash & Sampson
Total 33

Master Arthur Howe Esqr.
White Men: Arthur Howe
Negroe Men Slaves: Jack & Ben
Female Slaves: Pegg & Lucy
Total 5

Master Robt. Johnston
White Men: Robt. Johnston
Negro Men Slaves: Joe, Will, Jack & Harry
Female Slaves: Juno, Betty & Darcus
Boys Under Sixteen: Jamie
Total 9

Master Thos. Hall Esqr.
White Men: Thomas Hall Esqr.
Negro Men Slaves: Jery, Dartmouth, Sampson, Jamie, Prince, Gold, Jownsid[?], Billy, Quamino, Mars & Dover
Female Slaves: Eve, Sibill, Aba, Cynthia, Peggy, Penny, Daphne, Sinah, Hagar & Peggy
Boys Under Sixteen: Billy & Boatswain
Total 24

Master James Stewart
White Men: James Stewart
Negro Men Slaves: Don Carlos & Wilmot
Female Salves: Phillis
Total 4

Master Harbert Taylor
White Men: Harbert Taylor
Total [Not Given]

Master Doctr. Wm Bartram
White Men: William Bartram, John DuCamp, & Jeremiah Dafferd
Negro Men Slaves: Jack, Hope, Somp, Sampson, Longo & Cato
Female Slaves: Chloe, Belonda, Flora, Grace, Hannah & Amy
Boys Under Sixteen: Shiels, Benj. & Joe
Total 18

Master Archd. Schaw
White Men: Archd. Schaw
Total 1

****

BLADEN COUNTY TAX LIST OF 1770

A True List of Taxables taken by John Turner 1770

Headings for this list include: Whites, Black Males, Black Females, Above Sixty, Under Sixteen, & In All.

Whites: Taxables belonging to the Estate of Richd. Eagles & [Torn]mas Childs
Black Males: Lary, Toney, Joe, Andrew, Abraham, Billey, Charles, Ned, Dick, Sam, Dowey, Jammy, Cain, Montsaley
Black Females: Diannah, Amoritta, Alice, Sarah, Diannah, Doll, Phillis, Hager, Judah, Bettey, Sabinah, Kittey, Peggy, Nanney, Chloe, Sarah
Above Sixty: George, Prince, Simon
Under Sixteen: Ned
In All 36

Whites: John Gibbs Esqr.
Black Males: Ceasar, Peter, Sampson, Dennis & Tom
Black Females: Ameila, Juba, Bettey, Hannah, Judah, Nan & Chloe
Above Sixty: Johnney
In All 15

Whites: George Gibbs Esqr.
Black Males: Kent
Black Females: Eliza. K. Patrick, Diannah & Isabilla
Under Sixteen: Jammy, Jack
In All 7

Whites: James Lovel
Black Males: Hannabal
Black Females: Sarah, Grace
In All   4

Whites: Darby Murphey, John McClarin
In All   2

Whites: David [?], George Raybon
In All   2

Whites: Hugh Stewart
In All   1

Whites: John Cook
In All   1

Whites: Richard Rigel[?]
In All   1

Whites: William McNeal & David Bailey
Black Males: Mercury, Cambleton, & Duncan
Black Females: Chloe & Venus
In All   7

[The bottom of the above page is torn away & missing.]

Whites: James Baldwin
Black Males: Dublin
Black Females: Betty
In All   3

Whites: Daniel Shipman, James Shipman & Danl. Shipman Junr.
Black Males: Sam, & Ceasar
In All   5

Whites: Morris Biven & Thomas Jones
In All   2

Whites: Abraham Gray
In All   1

Whites: John Baldwin & [Faded] Baldwin
Black Males: Tincker, Tom, & Ben
Black Females: Abb & Pegg
In All   7

Whites: Joshua Hays Const.
Black Males: James
In All   2

Whites: John Powel Senr., Absalom Powel & John Powel
Black Males: Tom & Cyrus
Black Females: Frances
In All   6

Whites: James Dupre, Richd. Boyd & Robert Cohoon
Black Males: Francis
Black Females: Grace
In All   5

Whites: John Green
Black Females: Sabinah
In All   2

Whites: John Hilyard & John Hilyard Junr.
In All   2

Whites: Daniel Shaw
Black Females: Phebey
Under Sixteen: Lewis
In All   3

Whites: Isaac Wolf
In All   1

Whites: Benj. Beasley
In All   1

Whites: James Murphey
In All   1

Whites: Nathaniel Busby
In All   1

Whites: Thomas McClennen
In All   1

Whites: Daniel Turner
In All   1

Whites: John Green, William Green, & Simon Green
Black Males: Tom & Dick
Black Females: Tamer
Under Sixteen: Abraham
In All   7

Whites: William Green
In All   1

Whites: John McCowen, Robert McCowen, William McCown & John McClarin
In All   4

Whites: Jeremiah Bigfurd, Jeremiah Bigfurd &
William Bigfurd
Black Females: Affey
In All   4

Whites: Archibald McColsky, James McColsky
In All   2

[The bottom of the above page is torn away &
missing.]

Whites: Joseph Wiggans & Isham Wiggans
In All   2

Whites: Charles Raybon
In All   1

Whites: Francis Laron & William Register
In All   2

Whites: John Raybon
In All   1

Whites: John Stubbs & Richd. Stubbs
In All   2

Whites: Richd. Ridget
In All   1

Whites: Peter Simson
In All   1

Whites: Saml. Hughs, John Hughs & Malachi
Hughs
In All   3

Whites: Berry Wa[?]s
In All   1

Whites: Matthew Moore & Richd. Reynolds
Black Males: Allen Dimry & Peter
Black Females: Rose & Judah
In All   6

Whites: John Connolly
In All   1

Whites: Joseph Register
In All   1

Whites: Stephen Bryant
In All   1

Whites: Neal McCoulskey,
Patrole, Neal Shaw & Charles McNorton
Black Females: Phillis
Under Sixteen: Charles
In All   3

Whites: Isaac Green
Black Males: Greenidge, Ceasar, Quamino,
Cyrus & Damser
Black Females: Betty & Celia
Under Sixteen: Tom, James & Conely
In All   11

Whites: George Bruer[?]
In All   1

Whites: Zachar. Smith
Black Males: Dick
In All   2

Whites: John Green & James Gifferd
Black Males: Tom
In All   3

Whites: William Burny
Black Males: Sam & Jack
Black Females: Jane & Patt
In All   5

Whites: William Burny Jr.
In All   1

Whites: John Ellis, William Ellis, James Ellis &
Robert Ellis
Black Males: Dick & Joe
Black Females: Venus
Under Sixteen: Laurence
In All   8

Whites: John Cohoon
In All   1

Whites: James Cohoon
In All   1

Whites: Micajah Cohoon
In All   1

Whites: James Clardy & William Standfast
Black Males: Nat
In All   3

Whites: Saml. Rhuark Const.
Black Males: Cesor & Bob
In All   3

Chapter 3: Bladen County Tax Lists of 1770

Black Females: *Susannah Freeman & Rachel Freeman*
In All _____ 2

Whites: John McColskey
Black Males: Hamblet
In All _____ 2

Whites: James Green
Black Males: Daniel
In All _____ 2

Whites: Simon Brite &
Zacha. Brite
In All _____ 2

Whites: Simon Burny, Patrole
In All _____ 1

Whites: Alexander Stewart & John Kelly
Black Males: Robin
In All _____ 3

Whites: Matthew Kelly & John Barteries
Black Males: Limrick & Will
Black Females: Jude & Sall
In All _____ 6

Whites: John Campbell
In All _____ 1

Whites: Andrew McClennen & John McClennen
Black Females: Phebey
Under Sixteen: Cyrus
In All _____ 4

Whites: Daniel Norton, Jacob Norton & Miles Potter
In All _____ 3

Whites: William Bryant
Black Males: Jack
Under Sixteen: James
In All _____ 3

Whites: James Lewis & Solomon Lewis
In All _____ 2

Whites: Josiah Lewis & Josiah Lewis Jr.
Black Males: London
In All _____ 3

Whites: John Ethridge
In All _____ 1

Whites: Samuel Ethridge & Marmadk. Ethridge
Black Males: Jack
Black Females: Eve
In All _____ 4

Whites: Hanson Lewis & Josiah Lewis
Black Males: Will
Black Females: Patt
In All _____ 4

Whites: Jacob Norton
In All _____ 1

Whites: John Fokes, James Fokes & Jacob Fokes
In All _____ 3

Whites: John Ellis Junr.
In All _____ 1

Whites: Thomas Mims
Black Males: Tom
In All _____ 2

Whites: David Mims
In All _____ 1

Whites: William Barefoot
Black Males: Maby
In All _____ 2

Whites: Jessie Lancaster & Ralph Bowman
In All _____ 2

Whites: Benjamin Putnel
In All _____ 1

Whites: Benj. Lambethson & Richd. Lambethson
Black Males: Will & Jack
Black Females: Hannah, Sall, Doll & Jane
In All _____ 8

Whites: John Chancey & Zachry. Chancey
In All _____ 2

Whites: John Smith
In All _____ 1

Whites: John Tyson
In All _____ 1

Black Males: *A. Freeman, Saml. Freeman & RogerFreeman*
In All _____ 3

CHAPTER 4

BLADEN COUNTY TAX LISTS OF 1771

BLADEN COUNTY TAX LIST OF 1771

A True List of Taxables taken by John Turner forthe year 1771

Headings in this list include: **Whites, Black Males, Black Females, Above Sixty, Under Sixteen & In All.**

Whites: George Gibbs Esqr, John Forrester & Robert Stuart.
Black Males: Tony, Jack, Kent, Watty, Sam & James
Black Females: Deanah, Hannah, Bellah, Aminda, Sabina & Nanney
Under Sixteen: Jack & Tony
In All   17

Taxables belonging to the Estate of John Gibbs Esq. Deceased
Black Males: Ceasar, Johnny, Sampson, Peter, Buck Tom,Tom, Dennis & Bovan
Black Females: Eilza. Patrick, Amelia, Juba, Betty, Hannah, Judey, Nanny, Chloe & Clarinda
Under Sixteen: Jack
In All   18

Whites: Stephen Brittain
Black Males: Johnny, Jack, Jeffrey, Bass, Mingo, Cyrus, Jammy, Quash, Jackoe, Renty, Dancer, Quamino, Tom, Tom, Conner & Charles
Black Females: Cate, Cate, Peggey, Cumboe, Clarinda, Dianah, Delilah, Bellah & Bess
Under Sixteen: Fed
In All   27

Whites: John Turner & James Gifford
Black Males: London, Solomon, James, Ryall & Will
Black Females: Patience, Tam, Charlotte & u[Torn]
In All   11

Whites: Charles McNaughten
In All   1

Whites: James Murphey
In All   1

Whites: James Dupre, & Richard Boyd
Black Males: Frank
Black Females: Grace
In All   4

Whites: Nathaniel Beasely & Elisha Haygood
In All   2

Whites: John Conally
In All   1

Whites: Joseph Davis
In All   1

Whites: Joshua Hayse
In All   1

Whites: Daniel King
In All   1

Whites: John Raybon
In All   1

Whites: [Torn]ugall Blas[?]
In All   1

Whites: William McNeal, John White & Ebinezer Sweet
Black Males: Duncan, Mercury & Clyde
Black Females: Chloe & Ninus
In All   8

Whites: Anguish McCoye
In All   1

Whites: Charles Raybon
In All   1

Whites: Neal McCoulsky & Neal Shaw
Black Males: Charles
Black Females: Fillis
In All   4

Whites: Richard Ridgett
Black Females: Mary & Judy
In All   3

Whites: John Green
In All: 1

Whites: Daniel Turner
In All   1

Whites: John Dores[?] & William Starkey
In All   2

Whites: John Baldwin & Charles Baldwin
Black Males: Tinker, Tom & Ben
Black Females: Pigg & Aleb
Under Sixteen: Adam
In All   8

Whites: John McCown, Robt. McCown & Willm: McCown
In All   3

Whites: Josiah Lewis Senr. & Josiah Lewis Junr.
Black Males: London
In All   3

Whites: William Bryant
Black Males: Jack
In All   2

Whites: Simon Burney
In All   1

Whites: [Torn] Murphey, [Torn] McClaren & John McClaren
In All   3

Whites: James Lewis & Solomon Lewis
In All   2

Whites: James Lovet
Black Males: Hannabel
Black Females: Sarah & Grace
In All   4

Black Males: *Free Abe*
In All   1

Black Males: *Free Will*
In All   1

Black Males: *Free Roger*
In All   1

Black Females: *Free Sue*
In All   1

Black Females: *Free Rachael*
In All   1

Whites: John Ellis Senr., Robert Ellis, William Ellis & James Ellis
Black Males: Lawrence
Black Females: Venus
In All   6

Whites: Thomas Jones & Morris Biven
In All   2

Whites: John Smith & Stephen Smith
In All   2

Whites: Benjamin Arrington
Black Females: Poll
In All   2

Whites: Ezekiel Busbey
In All   1

Whites: Joseph Powers & Roger Neale
In All   2

Whites: Micajah Cahoon
In All   1

Whites: John Powell Senr., Absalom Powell & John Powell
Black Males: Sam & Cyrus
Black Female: Frank
In All   6

Whites: William Burney
Black Males: Sam & Jack
Black Females: Jane & Patt
In All   5

Whites: William Burney Jr.
In All   1

Whites: John Chancy & Zachariah Chancey
In All   2

Whites: James Cohoon
In All   1

Whites: William Boyte & Gabriel Parker
In All   2

Whites: John Cohoon
In All   1

Whites: John Fokes & Jacob Fokes
In All _____ 2

Whites: John Stubbs & Richard Stubbs
In All _____ 2

Whites: James Fokes
In All _____ 1

Whites: Zachariah Smith
Black Males: Dick
In All _____ 2

Whites: Danl. Shipman, Jas. Shipman Const. &
Danl. Shipman
Black Males: Sam & Ceasar
In All _____ 5

Whites: Simon Brite & Richard Brite
In All _____ 2

Whites: John Green, Simon Green & William
Green
Black Males: Tom & Dick
Black Females: Tamer
Under Sixteen: Abram
In All _____ 7

Whites: Robert Walker
In All _____ 1

Whites: Alexander Stewart
Black Females: Robin
In All _____ 2

Whites: Jeremiah Bigford Jr. & Jeremiah
Bigford
Black Females: Affry
In All _____ 3

Whites: Francis Lawson
In All _____ 1

Whites: Abraham Gray
In All _____ 1

Whites: John Cook
In All _____ 1

[Next line torn out] [Torn] Shaw
In All _____ 2

Whites: Matthew Kelly
Black Males: Limrick, Will & Jack
Black Females: Judey & Sall
In All _____ 7

Whites: Bryant Green
In All _____ 1

Whites: James Baldwin & Joseph Baldwin
Black Males: Dublin
Black Females: Betty
In All _____ 4

Whites: John Ellis
In All _____ 1

Whites: Archibald McCoulsky & Jas.
McCoulsky
Black Females: Chloe &
Eleanor
In All _____ 4

Whites: Andrew McCleland, John McCleland &
McClain McCleland
Black Females: Phebe
Under Sixteen: Cyrus
In All _____ 5

Whites: William Green
In All _____ 1

Whites: Benjamin Beasely
In All _____ 1

Whites: Isaac Wolf
In All _____ 1

Whites: Joseph Wiggans
In All _____ 1

Whites: Handson Lewis & Josiah Lewis
Black Males: Will
Black Females: Patt
In All _____ 4

Whites: John Bistros
In All _____ 1

Whites: James Green
Black Males: Daniel
In All _____ 2

Whites: William Barefoot
Black Males: Maybe
In All _____ 2

Whites: Thomas Mims
Black Males: Tom
In All   2

Whites: David Mims
In All   1

Whites: Benja. Lambethson, Richd. Lambethson
Black Males: Will & Jack
Black Females: Hannah, Sall, Jane & Doll
In All   8

Whites: George Bruer & William Bruer
In All   2

Whites: John Hillyard Sr. & John Hillyard Jr.
In All   2

Whites: William White
Black Males: Quaco
Black Females: Sall
In All   3

Whites: James Clardy & William Standfast
Black Males: Quash, Boson & Natt
In All   5

Whites: Samuel Rhuark
Black Males: Ceasar & Bob
In All   3

Whites: Matthew Moore & Micajah Johnston
Black Males: Allen Dimory & Peter
Black Females: Rose & Jude
In All   6

****

BLADEN COUNTY TAX
LIST OF 1771

August 1771 Peter Lord[?] List of Taxables

Headings in this list include: Whites, Black Men, Black Women, Boys & Girls & Total.

Whites: Henerey Messen
Total   1

Whites: David Young
Total   1

Whites: Jacob Taler & William Taler
Black Men: Will
Total   3

Whites: Oxford Beasley & James Beasley
Total   2

Whites: Richard Elwell
Black Men: Harry
Boys & Girls: Fanney
Total   3

Whites: John McCain
Total   1

Whites: William Lee
Total   1

Whites: Duncan Campbell & Hugh Campbell
Black Men: Cuff
Total   3

Whites: Hector McNeal
Black Men: Gragg
Black Women: Nan
Total   3

Whites: James McNeal
Black Men: Tom & Tony
Black Women: Cait
Total   4

Whites: Donnel Paterson
Total   1

Whites: Donnel Mcafee & Archable
Total   2

Whites: John Bohand & John Dorman
Total   2

Whites: Archable Little
Total   1

Whites: Duncan Little
Total   1

Whites: Philip T. Kne[?] & son Mickall
Total   2

Whites: Alexander Little
Total   1

Whites: John Johnson
Total   1

Whites: Duncan Bosey
Total   1

Chapter 4: Bladen County Tax Lists of 1771

Whites: William Kirkpatrick
Black Men: Toby
Black Women: Dianah
Total   3

Whites: James Jackson
Total   1

Whites: Elias Stone & Son David & James
Total   3

Whites: Joseph Cooper & Ben[?]
Black Men: Cuff & Prince
Total   4

Whites: Edmondson Wear[?]
Black Men: Coley, Quash
[Torn]
Black Women: Moll
Total   6

Whites: Agerton Willis & Benjamin [Torn]
Benjamin [?], James Moore, Agerton
Mout[Moor?]
Black Men: 10
Black Women: 7
Boys & Girls: 10
Total   33

Whites: Robert Upton & David Upton
Total   2

Whites: Neal McNeal
Total   1

Whites: John Lock & son John
Black Men: Sesen
Black Women: Murtilar
Boys & Girls: Vilet & Jacob
Total   7

Whites: James Elles & Thomas Moor
Black Men: Dick, Prince & Zo[?] Bristo
Black Women: Sinah
Boys & Girls: John & Blank[Torn]
Total   8

Whites: Levey Ennis
Total   1

Whites: Samuel Beltman
Total   1

Whites: Isaiah Powell
Total   1

Whites: John Shoester
Total   1

Whites: Abell Corbet
Total   1

Whites: John Berry
Total   1

Whites: Lewes Munroe
Black Men: Jamey
Total   2

Whites: John Legeth & Richard Wilkson
Black Men: 1
Black Women: 1
Total   4

Whites: Michael Kasters
Total   1

Whites: Lennard Lock
Black Men: Quash
Black Females: Grass
Total   3

Whites: Joseph Thims & Son Tessey
Total   2

Whites: William Donnahow & William Collins
Total   2

Whites: George T Ikner; constable & John
Williams
Black Men: York
Total   3

Whites: John Storm
Total   1

Whites: Samuel Cannedy & son Jacob
Black Men: Charles
Black Women: Paney
Total   4

Whites: Andrew Puff
Total   1

Whites: Donnel McTager
Total   1

Whites: Britan Barns
Total   1

Chapter 4:   Bladen County Tax Lists of 1771

Whites: Samuel Cannedy
Total _____ 1

Whites: Tobias Sealey
Total _____ 1

Whites: John N O'berry Junr.
Black Men: Quash & Makas
Black Females: Freles
Total _____ 4

Whites: James Marsh
Total _____ 1

Whites: Samuel Butler & Stephen Butler
Black Men: Cob, Sam, Come & Harey
Black Women: Cess
Total _____ 7

Whites: William Moor & son Matthew & John
Total _____ 3

Whites: William Moor Junr.
Total _____ 1

Whites: Robert Sims
Total _____ 1

Whites: James Moor & James Rising
Total _____ 2

Whites: William Malspy & brother Samuel
Total _____ 2

Whites: James Simms & sons Isaac & James Simms & Peter Hamblton
Boys & Girls: harey
Total _____ 5

Whites: [Torn]essey Newberry
Black Men: Quash, Sam, Tom, York & Dick
Black Women: Judy
Total _____ 7

Whites: John Newberry Senr.
Black Women: Dinah
Total _____ 2

Whites: John Moor & James Moor
Total _____ 2

Whites: Uriah Lamburd
Total _____ 1

Whites: Benjamin Simms & Joseph Hogs
Total _____ 2

Whites: Thomas Ackson[?]
Total _____ 1

Whites: Peter Carpenter
Total _____ 1

Whites: John Purnall
Total _____ 1

Whites: Levey Glass
Black Men: Ned
Black Women: Betey & Bet
Total _____ 4

Whites: Solomon Wilson
Total _____ 1

Whites: Thomas Robeson Esq. & Barten De[?]
Black Men: 2
Black Women: 3
Total _____ 7

Whites: Joseph Price
Total _____ 1

Whites: Morgan Drury
Total _____ 1

****

BLADEN COUNTY TAX LIST OF 1771

1771

Headings in this list include: **Whites, Blacks, Wenches, Boys Under 16, Fellows Above 16, Carriages, Wheels & Total.**

Berringer Moore
Whites: 1
Blacks 4
Wenches: 6
Boys Under 16: 2
Fellows Above 16: 2
Carriages: 1
Wheels: 2
Total 13

Marmaduke Jones
Whites: 2
Blacks: 16
Wenches: 13
Boys Under 16: 1
Fellows Above 16: 2
Carriages: 1
Wheels: 2
Total 34

Thomas McGuire
Whites: 2
Blacks: 15
Wenches: 18
Boys Under 16: 3
Carriages: 2
Wheels: 6
Total: 38

John Campbell
Whites: 1
Blacks: 20
Wenches: 18
Boys Under 16: 4
Total: 43

Mary Newton
Blacks: 5
Wenches: 2
Total: 7

Aron Dardy
Whites: 1
Blacks: 1
Total 2

John Smith
Whites: 1
Total 1

Daniel Curry
Whites: 1
Total: 1

Charles Benbow
Whites: 4
Wenches: 1
Boys Under 16: 1
Total: 6

Thomas Chiles
Whites: 1
Blacks: 8
Wenches: 6
Total: 15

John Jones
Whites: 1
Blacks: 1
Wenches: 3
Total: 5

****

BLADEN COUNTY TAX LIST OF 1771

A True List of Taxables for the year 1771 Taken Before me Archd. McKissaks J.P.

Headings in this list include: Whites, Blacks, Molatoes & No.

Molatoes: 3
Daniel Wharton & Wife & son Daniel
No. 3

Whites
Archd. McLean 1
No. 1

Whites
Abram Paul as Const. 1
No. 1

Whites
James Wilkinson 1
No. 1

Whites
Archd. Thompson 1
No. 1

Whites
Daniel McLean & Archd. McCurtan 2
Blacks: Negro Boye Dan
No. 3

Whites
Thomas Sterling & Son Thos. 2
No. 2

Molatoes 3
John Lockliar & wife & son Wm. 3
No. 3

Whites
John McCraine & son in law Daniel McLauchlan
& Allan Mcafie 3
No. 3

Whites
Hugh McCraine & son Hugh   2
Blacks: Negro Fellow Tony & a Wench warry.
                                               2
No.   4

Whites
Malcom Munroe   1
No.   1

Whites
John Mcfaul & son Neill   2
Blacks: Negroe felloe Briggie & wenches Fany
& Sarah   3
No.   5

Whites
Hugh Brown   1
Blacks: negroe wench Sall   1
No.   2

Whites
Peter & Neill McCarter   2
No.   2

Whites
Neill McNeill, John Hart & Hector McNeill
sailor   3
Blacks: negroe fellow peter
No.   4

Whites
George Colly & Joshua Harp   2
No.   2

Whites
James Furguarson   1
No.   1

Whites
Turkel McNeill son Lauchland & Gilbert
McaNewer[?]   3
Blacks: Negroe fellows fortune, old & young
Jack, frank & wenches Rose & Bett   6
No.   9

Whites
John Paul   1
No.   1

Whites
Edward & Thursbee Brown   2
No.   2

Molatoes   1
Charles Oxendine
No.   1

Whites
Carraway Oates   1
No.   1

Whites
William Grantham & brother John   2
No.   2

Whites
Edward Grantham   1
Blacks: negroe fellow
hampton   1
No.   2

Whites
Tarlo oqwinn & son John   2
No.   2

Whites
Richd. Smith   1
Blacks: negroe wench Chloe   1
No.   2

Whites
William Butler   1
No.   1

Whites
Joseph Milton   1
No.   1

Whites
Moses Grice & Brother Robert   2
No.   2

Whites
Samson Pittman & Hardy oqwinn   2
No.   2

Whites
Jacob Pittman   1
No.   1

Whites
Jacob Alford   1
No.   1

Whites
Thos. Talton Junr. & Brother Jas.   2
No.   2

Whites
William Gulledge as Cons.   1
No.   1

Whites
Samuel Strikland   1
No.   1

Molatoes   2
James Lowry & Wm. Jones
Blacks: Negroe fellow Jack   1
No.   3

Molatoes   1
Ishmael Cheves
No.   1

Molatoes   1
Jacob Lockliar
No.   1

Whites
Thos. Bullard   1
No.   1

Whites
Ambrous Bullard   1
No.   1

Whites
Aaron Strikland   1
No.   1

Whites
Abram Strikland   1
No.   1

Whites
Thomas Bryan   1
No.   1

Whites
William Taylor   1
No.   1

Whites
Elizabeth Best & sons John & Bryan Best   2
No.   2

Whites
Isaac Wilks & James Sutton   2
No.   2

Whites
Malcom Buye   1
Blacks: negroe boy Will   1
No.   2

Whites
Malcom Campbell   1
No.   1

Whites
Demsey Bairfield   1
No.   1

Whites
Henry Smith   1
No.   1

Whites
David Williams   1
No.   1

Whites
William Jones   1
No.   1

Whites
John Duncan   1
No.   1

Whites
Smith   1
No.   1

Molatoes   1
Cannon Cumbo
No.   1

Whites
Moses Cox   1
No.   1

Molatoes   2
Ann Perkins Taxables Thos. Sweat & her son
Jordan Perkins
No.   2

Whites
Elisha Sweetin   1
Blacks: negroe girl Pegg   1
No.   2

Whites
John Bues   1
No.   1

Molatoes		1
Thomas Groome		
No.		1

Whites		
Tarlor oqwinn Junr.		1
No.		1

Molatoes		2
John & Neill Rouse		
No.		2

Whites		
William Wilkinson & son Wm.		2
No.		2

Whites		
John Branch		1
No.		1

Whites		
James Johnston		1
Blacks: negroe wench Anaca		1
No.		2

Whites		
Britain Branch		1
No.		1

Whites		
Lewis Hall & son Lewis & Isaac Hall Senr.		3
No.		3

Whites		
Enoch Hall		1
No.		1

Whites		
Isaac Hall		1
No.		1

Whites		
John Fiveash & son Demsey		2
No.		2

Whites		
Benjamin Fuller		1
Blacks: negroe wench patt		1
No.		2

Whites		
Thomas Bud		1
No.		1

Molatoes		2
Jas. Doyal & wife		
No.		2

Whites		
John Gibson		1
Blacks: Negroe fellow Kalis & wenches Lucy & Pleasant		3
No.		4

Blacks: John Cades Negroe wench Nell		1
No.		1

Whites		
Abram Barnes Esqr.		1
Blacks: Negroe wench Sall[?] & Negroe boy Jack Taken by Esqr. Barnes		2
No.		3

Whites		
Ignasious Flowers		1
No.		1

Whites		
Thos. Brown Senr. & son Thos.		2
Blacks: Negroe wench Pender		1
No.		3

Whites		
Thos. Stevens		1
No.		1

Whites		
Charles Bairfield		1
No.		1

Molatoes		2
Solomon Johnston & wife		
No.		2

Whites		
John Cairsey & son Jacob		2
Molatoes		1
William Horn		
Blacks: Negroe wench Abb		1
No.		4

Molatoes		1
Thos. Cairsey Junr.		
No.		1

Molatoes		2
[Torn] *Goen & wife*		
No.		2

Chapter 4: Bladen County Tax Lists of 1771

Molatoes 3
Richd Wharton & wife & Jacob Braveboy
No. 3

Whites
Richd. Grantham 1
No. 1

Whites
Jas. Grantham 1
No. 1

Whites
Joseph Price & son in Law Reuben Roberts 2
No. 2

Whites
Shadrach Baget 1
No. 1

****

BLADEN COUNTY TAX LIST OF 1771

Joseph Clark Esqr. List of Taxables for the Year 1771

Headings in this list include: Whites, Mulatoes, Black Males, Black Females & Total.

Whites: Wm. Bartram, Jno. Ducamp & Jeremiah Dafferd[?] 3
Black Males 9
Black Females 6
Total 18

Whites: Archabald Baxter 1
Total 1

Whites: John Boyd Senr. & Junr. & Charles Orr 3
Black Females 1
Total 4

Whites: Dugald Blue 1
Total 1

Whites: Benoni Clayton 1
Total 1

Whites: William Davis 1
Total 1

Whites: Archa. Darrah, Jno. White & Jno. Roberts 3
Black Males 1
Total 4

Whites: William Forrester 1
Total 1

Whites: Bryan Green & Jno Holland 2
Total 2

Whites: John Grange, Thomas & Jno. Conner 3
Black Males 13
Black Females 17
Total 33

Whites: Moses Ho[Faded]es 1
Total 1

Whites: Wm. How 1
Total 1

Whites: Arthur How 1
Black Males 2
Black Females 2
Total 5

Whites: Thomas Hall 1
Black Males 13
Black Females 10
Total 24

Whites: John Jones 1
Black Males 2
Black Females 2
Total 5

Whites: Thomas Jones 1
Total 1

Whites: Robert Johnston 1
Black Males 5
Black Females 3
Total 9

Whites: Jno. Lucas, Jesse Oliphan & Jas. Carver 3
Black Males 8
Black Females 5
Total 16

Whites: Jacob Messik 1
Total 1

Whites: Ralph Miller Senr. & Junr. & James
Morrison   3
Black Males   3
Black Females   3
Total   9

Whites: Daniel & Archabald McFarter   2
Total   2

Whites: Iever McKay   1
Black Males   2
Black Females   3
Total   6

Whites: Daniel McFarter   1
Total   1

Whites: Duncan McKeithan   1
Black Males   1
Total   2

Whites: Archa. & Malcom McBride   2
Total   2

Whites: Ann Maultsby & sons Jas. & Saml. 2
Black Males   1
[Torn]   [Torn]

Whites: Saml. McRee   1
[Torn & Faded]

Whites: Archa. McKeithan   1
[Torn & Faded]

Whites: John Oder[n?]   1
[Torn & Faded]

Whites: John Pointer Senr. & Junr. & Richd.
Mullington   3
[Torn & Faded]

Whites: John & James Pemperton   2
Black Males   1
[Torn & Faded]

Whites: Jonadab Russ   1
[Torn & Faded]

Whites: Richd., Benja. & Wm Singletary 3
Black Males   4
Black Females   1
Total   8

Whites: Wm & John Smith   2
Black Males   2
Total   4

Whites: Neill Schaw & son Alexr. & Christr.
Goodon   3
Black Males   2
Black Females   1
Total   6

Whites: Richd. Small & Jno. Young   2
Total   2

Whites: Jno. & Malcom Schaw   2
Total   2

Whites: John Small Constable   0
Total   0

Whites: James Stewart   1
Black Males   2
Black Females   1
Total   4

Whites: Archa. Schaw   1
Total   1

Whites: Harbert Taylor   1
Total   1

Whites: John Wolf & Mathew Parker   2
Total   2

Whites: Stephen White   1
Total   1

Whites: Col. Hugh Waddell & Overseer   2
Black Males   17
Black Females   16
Total   35

****

BLADEN COUNTY TAX LIST OF 1771

William McRee Esqr List of Taxables 1771

**Headings for this list include: Whites,
Mulatoes, Black Males, Black Females, Boys,
Wheels & Total.**

Whites: George Brown Esqr & Thomas & John
                                              3
Black Males   1
Black Females   3
Boys   2
Total   9

Whites: John Bentley	1
Total	1

Whites: Philoman Bryan and son Philoman	2
Black Females	1
Total	3

Whites: John Bryan & William Doulas	2
Black Females	1
Total	3

Whites: Stephen Bryan	1
Total	1

Whites: Thomas Bryan Exempted	0
Black Males	1
Total	1

Whites: Edward and David Bryan	2
Black Males	1
Total	3

Whites: Emey Bryan	0
Black Males	1
Black Females	2
Total	3

Whites: Samuel Cu[?]	1
Total	1

Whites: Maturin Colvill	1
Black Males	2
Black Females	2
Boys	1
Total	6

Whites: John Dryden	1
Total	1

Whites: Charles Dent	1
Total	1

Whites: Samuel Evers, William [Torn]	[Torn]
	3
Total	3

Whites: Samuel Gaston	1
Total	1

Whites: Benjamin Humphrys	1
Total	1

Whites: John Hill	1
Total	1

Whites: Elizabeth Harrison with Two sons Jno & Edward	2
Black Males	1
Black Females	1
Boys	1
Total	5

Whites: Stephen Hester	1
Total	1

Whites: William Handen	1
Black Males	1
Black Females	1
Total	3

Whites: Jesse Howard	1
Total	1

Whites: I.I.W. Hester, Wm. Hester constable, Jno. Aaron Moore & William Morris	4
Total	4

Whites: Dennis Lennon	1
Black Males	2
Total	3

Whites: John Lemon	1
Black Females	1
Total	2

Whites: Jacob Muns	1
Total	1

Whites: John McLauchland	1
Total	1

Whites: Robert McConkey	1
Black Males	1
Black Female	1
Total	3

Whites: John Russ & son John	2
Total	2

Whites: David Russ	1
Total	1

Whites: John Simpson Senr. & John Simpson Junr.	2
Total	2

Whites: William Singletary	1
Black Males	1
Black Females	1
Total	3

Whites: Joseph, Braton & William Singletary
                                          3
Black Males   1
Black Females   1
Total   5

Whites: David White   1
Black Males   2
Total   3

Whites: Stephen White & James Erwin 2
Total   2

****

BLADEN COUNTY TAX LIST OF 1771

Thomas Robeson Esqr List of Taxables for the Year 1771

Headings for this list include: Whites, Free Negroes & Molatoes, Black Male Slaves, Black Females, Boys Under Sixteen, Carriage Wheels & Total.

Whites: William Anderson   1
Total   1

Whites: John Anderson   1
Total   1

Whites: Andrew Andruss   1
Total   1

Whites: Margaret Byrne   1
Black Male Slaves: 4
Black Females   3
Total   8

Whites: Robert Baker   1
Black Male Slaves: 1
Total   2

Whites: Joseph Butler   1
Black Male Slaves   2
Total   3

Whites: Laurence Byrne & 3 sons   4
Total   4

Whites: Daniel Beard   1
Total   1

White: Neill Beard & son & Grandson 3
Black Male Slaves   1
Total   4

Whites: James Bennet & Samuel Hales 2
Total   2

Whites: John & Holton Beard   2
Total   2

Whites: James Baily [**Basly?**], Neill McDuffie, Jas. Smith & William Smith 4
Black Male Slaves   6
Black Females   5
Total   15

Whites: William Braford   1
Total   1

Whites: Joseph Cain   1
Black Male Slaves   1
Black Females   1
Total   3

Whites: Richd. Chesher & Peter Matax 2
Total   2

Whites: Joseph Carter & son   2
Total   2

Whites: Samuel Cain   1
Black Male Slaves   1
Total   2

Whites: William Cain, son & *Free Jamey*[?]
                                         2
Free Negroes & Mulatoes   1
Black Male Slaves   5
Black Females   3
Total   11

Whites: William Cain [**Cairne**] & two sons 3
Total   3

Whites: Benjamin Clark & 2 sons   3
Total   3

Whites: Benjamin Clark   1
Black Male Slaves   1
Black Females   1
Total   3

Whites: Edward Davis   1
Black Females   1
Total   2

Whites: Baxter Davis & John Bedsole 2
Total   2

Whites: John Davis	1
<u>Total</u>	1

Whites: John Edmison	1
Black Females	1
<u>Total</u>	2

Whites: Robert Edward	1
Black Male Slaves	2
<u>Total</u>	3

Whites: Stephen Freeman	1
<u>Total</u>	1

Whites: John & Peter Gates	2
<u>Total</u>	2

Whites: Andrew Graham	1
<u>Total</u>	1

Whites: John Green	1
Black Females	1
<u>Total</u>	2

Whites: Robert Grice	1
<u>Total</u>	1

Whites: Josiah Handen Senr. & Jacob Gaston [Gayton]	3
Black Male Slaves	2
<u>Total</u>	5

Whites: Josiah Handen Junr.	1
Black Male Slaves	2
Black Females	1
<u>Total</u>	4

Whites: Mathew Higgens	1
Black Male Slaves	1
<u>Total</u>	2

Whites: Stephen Hollingsworth & son Isaac	2
<u>Total</u>	2

Whites: John Hollingsworth	1
<u>Total</u>	1

Whites: John Jervise	1
<u>Total</u>	1

Whites: Isaac Jessup	1
<u>Total</u>	1

Free Negroes & Mulatoes	2
John Johnston & Wife	
<u>Total</u>	2

Whites: Josiah Johnston	1
<u>Total</u>	1

Whites: William Johnston & 2 Sons & Wm Bigford	4
<u>Total</u>	4

Whites: Samuel Jones	1
<u>Total</u>	1

Whites: Thomas Jones	1
<u>Total</u>	1

****

BLADEN COUNTY TAX LIST OF 1771

George Brown Esqr List of Taxables 1771

Headings in this list include: Whites, Free Negroes & Mulatoes, Black Males, Black Females, Boys, Carages & Total.

Whites: Thomas Anderson & William Townsend	2
<u>Total</u>	2

Whites: Thomas Avery	1
<u>Total</u>	1

Whites: William Avery	1
<u>Total</u>	1

Whites: Lewis Avery	1
<u>Total</u>	1

Whites: Samuel Boazman	1
<u>Total</u>	1

Whites: Joseph Camp	1
Black Females	1
<u>Total</u>	2

Whites: James & Thomas Coopland	2
<u>Total</u>	2

Whites: Dennis Collum	1
<u>Total</u>	1

Whites: Even Ellis	1
Black Males	1
Black Females	1
<u>Total</u>	3

Whites: William Ellis	1
Total	1

Whites: John & Thomas Grange	2
Black Males	11
Black Females	15
Boys	2
Total	30

Whites: John Harrison & James Issom	2
Black Males	1
Total	3

Whites: Alexander Harvey	1
Total	1

Whites: Richard Harrison	1
Black Males	1
Total	2

Whites: Isaac Jones & Edwd & Jos Humphreys	3
Black Males	3
Black Females	2
Total	8

Whites: Ephram Lennon	1
Total	1

Whites: Robert & William McRee[?]	2
Total	2

Whites: William Owens	1
Black Males	1
Black Females	1
Total	3

Whites: Richard Satter, John Stone & Jas. Fason	3
Black Males	1
Boys	3
Total	7

Whites: John Smith & sons Wm. & Sam: & Wm. Haregrove	4
Black Males	5
Black Females	4
Boys	1
Total	14

Whites: Thomas Townsend	1
Total	1

Whites: [Torn] [Torn] & Hugh Porter	2
Black Males	2
Total	4

Whites: [Torn] [Torn] Senr. & Mathew	2
Black Males	1
Black Females	2
Total	5

Whites: John White Junr.	1
Black Males	1
Total	2

Whites: William White	1
Black Males	1
Black Females	1
Total	3

Whites: David White	1
Total	1

Free Negroes & Mulatoes	2
Moses Walker & Wife	
Total	2

****

BLADEN COUNTY TAX LIST OF 1771

A List of Taxables taken by David Morley for the [Year] 1771

Headings in this list include: Whites. The second heading is not given, but it is for Slaves.

Whites: Henry Bozell	1

Whites: Christopher Saunders	1

Whites: Thomas Browder	1

Whites: John Clark	1
Slaves: Scipio & Sue	2

Whites: Nathan Jones	1

Whites: Israel Tomkins, Aaron Tomkins & Lidia Tomkins	2
Slaves	1

Whites: Thomas Saunders, & William Saunders	2
Slaves: Tom & Frank	2

Whites: Thos. Johnson 1
Slaves: July 1

Whites: James Money & Benjamin Money 2

Whites: William Johnson & son John 2

Whites: Barnabas Stephens 1
Slaves 4

Whites: David Duncan 2
Slaves 2

Whites: John Busby & 2 sons 3

Whites: Edward Wall 1

Whites: George Duke 1

Whites: Ezekiel Hill 3

Whites: Miles Busby 2

Whites: Arthur Jones 1

Whites: John Baldwin 1
Slaves 2

Whites: William Horn 1
Slaves 1

Whites: Stephen Marlow 1

Whites: Abraham Danford 1

Whites: Daniel McNichols & Thomas
McNichols 2

Whites: John Carlisle 1

Whites: Thomas Bourn & three sons 4

Whites: Joshuway [?] 1
Slaves 2

Whites: Jacob [Faded] 1

****

BLADEN COUNTY TAX LIST OF 1771

Constable David Morley:s List of Taxables taken By George Gibbs

Headings in this list include: Whites & Slaves.

[This first entry doesn't make much sense.]

Whites: David Morley 1
Will 2
Sarah 4

Whites: Southey Hays 1

Whites: Thomas Dyson & Jack Walters 2

Whites: Thomas Hays 1

Whites: Moses [Faded] 1

Whites: John Yeates 1

Whites: John Butler 1

Whites: Thomas Hardwick & two Sons 3

Whites: John Johnson 1

Whites: Benedick Williams 1

Whites: Alexander Stevenson 1

Whites: Daniel Flinn 1

Whites: Edward Willson 2

Whites: John Wilson Senr. 1

Whites: Luke [Faded] 1

Whites: William Strikland 1
Slaves 1

Whites: James Willson 1

Whites: Abraham King 2

Whites: John Simpson, David Clark & 1 Negroe
2
Slaves 1

Whites: John Williams & Joshua Williams 2

Whites: William Rains 1

Whites: George Clark 1

Whites: William Brown 1

Whites: William Stevens 1

Whites: Balitha Hays 2

Chapter 4:   Bladen County Tax Lists of 1771

Whites: John Rogers	1
Whites: Joseph Noble	1
Whites: Jacob Hanchee[?]	1
Whites: Joseph Sims	2
Whites: Joseph Adams	1
Whites: John Brantor [Brantford]	1
Whites: John G Oyard	1
Slaves	1
Whites: Caleb Caloway	1

The following list seems to be a rough draft of the preceding two lists.

A List of Taxables Taken by David Morley for the Year 1771

There are no headings given for this list.

Henry Bozel	1
Kitt Sanders Constable	1
Thos Browder	1
John Clark	1
Scipio & Sue	2
Nathan Jones	1
Israel Tomkins, and Wife Lidia	2
Thomas Sanders, sons William & Thomas	3
Frank	1
Thos Johnson	1
July	1
James Money & Brother Benjamin	2
William Johnson & son John	2
Barnabas Stevens	1
Slaves	1
David Duncan	2
Slaves	2

John Busby & 2 sons	3
Edward Wall	1
George Duke	1
Ezekiel Hill	3
Miles Busby	2
Arthur Jones	1
John Baldwin	1
Slaves	2
William Horn	1
Slaves	1
Stephen Marlow	1
Abraham Danford	1
Danl McNichols and Son Thomas	2
Suthey Hays	1
Thos Dyson & Jack Walters	2
Sol Dyson	1
Thos Hays	1
Moses Coleman	1
James Brown	1
John Yeates	1
John Butler	1
Thos Hardwick and two Sons	3
John Johnson	1
Benedick Williams	1
Alexander Stevenson	1
Daniel Flinn	1
Edward Wilson	2
John Wilson Senr	1

Chapter 4:   Bladen County Tax Lists of 1771

Luke Barfield	1
Slaves	5
William Strikland	1
Slaves	1
James Wilson	1
Aberham King	2
John Simpson & David Clark	2
Slaves	1
John Williams & JoshuawayWilliams	2
William Rains	1
George Clark	1
William Brown	1
William Stevens	1
Berlitha Hays & John Rogers	2
John Carlisle	1
Joseph Noble	1

****

BLADEN COUNTY TAX LIST OF 1771

A list of the inhabitance within my District July 18th 1771 Peter Carpenter

There are no headings in this list.

William Salter
Walter Gibson
David Lloyd
David Lock Sinr.
Samuel McRee
Daniel McCloud
Brayton Singletary
Elizabeth Singletary
Joseph Lock
Thomas Lucus
Sarath Wilson
Jno Kannon[?]
Ephram Lennon
Jessy Blackwell
Hezekiah Davis
James Benson
James Dowey

Richard Huffaim
Hudling Huffaim
George Thomas Sinr.
George Thomas Jur.
Jessy Oliphant
Roger Neil
Benjamin Purnal[?]
Archabel Campill
Thomas Russ
Ephram Mulfort
William Davis
Jno Davis

[Rest of this document is torn away.]

****

BLADEN COUNTY TAX LIST OF 1771

A List of the Masters of Famailys Summoned Agreeable to a warrant to me Directed for that Purpose

There are no headings for this list.

Morgan Druit
Godfry McNeill
John McFarson
James Ard
Mash William Moore Senr
Mash William Moore Junr
Green Bodiford
William Hubbard
Isaac Kennady
Isaac Rozar
Jesse Moss
John Rozar
John Lee
Thomas Jackson
Jesse Muselwhite
William Ard
John Baxley
William Baxley
Great swamp William Moore
Benjamin Britt Junr
Geor[g]e Harrell
Thomas Little
Thomas Muselwhite
Chambers Humphreys
John Hammon
Lewis Jenkins
Joseph Mercer
John Blount
Jacob Blount
James Blount Junr.
John Edens

70

Solomon Mercer Junr.
Peter Lewis
Joseph Regan
Ralph Regan
John Regan
Solomon Mercer Senr.
Philip Blount
Joseph Baggett
Samuel Edwards
Samuel Andrews
English Thomas Jackson
Reuben Roberts
William Worrell
Henry Pope
Henry Bird
Thos Russel
Thomas Ivey
David Braveboy
Solomon Whitley
William Freeman
Henry Taylor
Benjamin Freeman
Peter Carsey
John Bullard
John Wilson
Thos Carsey Senr.
George Young Senr.
George Young Junr
Ambrus Powel
Charles Powel
William Singleton
James Blount Senr
Thomas Creel

The above Named Persons Duly Summoned Pr me Lazarus Creel Constable: Sworn before me this 3 of August 1771 Abram Barors[?]

****

BLADEN COUNTY TAX LIST OF 1771

A list of Taxabells taken for the year 1771 Pr Wm McRee

Headings in this list include: Whites, Men Slaves, Women Slaves, Boys & C & Total.

Whites: Maturin Colvill	1
Men Slaves	2
Women Slaves	1
Boys &C	2
Total	6

Whites: John Drydan	1
Total	1

Whites: George Brown, Thos and John	3
Men Slaves	1
Women Slaves	3
Boys &C	2
Total	9

Whites: John Bentley	1
Total	1

Whites: Denis Lennon	1
Men Slaves	2
Total	3

Whites: John Lennon	1
Women Slaves	1
Total	2

Whites: Jacob Muns	1
Total	1

Whites: John Simpson & John Simson	2
Total	2

Whites: Philemon Bryan Senr & Philemon Bryan Junr	2
Women Slaves	1
Total	3

Whites: John McGlacklain	1
Total	1

Whites: Saml Evers	1
Total	1

Whites: Benjm. Humphrey	1
Total	1

Whites: Robert McConkey	1
Men Slaves	1
Women Slaves	1
Total	3

Whites: John Bryan & Wm Dowlas	2
Women Slaves	1
Total	3

Whites: John Hill	1
Total	1

Whites: Elizabeth Harrison, John Harison & Edwd Harison	2
Men Slaves	1
Women Slaves	1
Boys &C	1

Whites: Stephen Bryan 1
Total 1

Whites: Stephen Hestors 1
Total 1

Whites: John Russ & son John Russ 2
Total 2

Whites: Wm. Singletary 1
Men Slaves 1
Women Slaves 1
Total 3

Whites: Joseph Singletary & sons Brayton & Wm. 3
Men Slaves 1
Women Slaves 1
Total 5

Whites: Charles Dent 1
Total 1

Whites: Thomas Bryant Exempt
Boys &C 1
Total 1

Whites: Edwd. Bryant & David Bryant 2
Men Slaves 1
Total 3

Whites: Amey Bryan
Women Slaves 2
Boys &C 1
Total 3

Whites: David Russ 1
Total 1

Whites: Samuel Gyton[?], Wm. and Edmond Russ 3
Total 3

Whites: David White 1
Men Slaves 2
Total 3

Whites: Wm. Henden 1
Men Slaves 1
Women Slaves 1
Total 3

Whites: Samuel Curry 1
Total 1

Whites: Jesse Howard 1
Total 1

Whites: Thomas Hestor, Wm Hestor Constable, John Hestor, Arron Moor & Thomas Moris 4
Total 4

Whites: Stephen White and James Ervin 2
Total 2

****

BLADEN COUNTY TAX LIST OF 1771

A List of Taxables returned to August Court 1771

The within List taken by me and returned to August Court 1771 Jos. Clarke

Headings in this list include: Masters & Mistresses, White Taxables, Men Slaves, Negro Women & Boys.

Masters & Mistresses: Jacob Messick
White Taxables: Jacob Messick Senr. & Jacob Messick Junr 2

Masters & Mistresses: Iver McKay
White Taxables: Iver Mackay 1
Men Slaves: Caesar & Anthony 2
Negro Women: Phillis & Dianah 2

Masters & Mistresses: John Pointer
White Taxables: John Pointer Senr., Richard Millington, John Pointer Junr. & Argalus Pointer 4
Men Slaves: Caesar & Fortune 2
Negro Women: Moll 1

Masters & Mistresses:
William Davis
White Taxables: William Davis 1

Masters & Mistresses:
William Smith
White Taxables: William Smith, John Smith & William Smith Junr 3
Men Slaves: Will & Prince 2

Masters & Mistresses: John Lucas
White Taxables: John Lucas, John Lucas Junr & James Carver   3
Men Slaves: Will, Tony, Caesar, Roger, Prince & Duck   6
Negro Women: Sue, Moll, Lucy, Cate & Lettice   5
Boys: Peter & Will   2

Masters & Mistresses: Sarah Seimour
White Taxables: Tom Seimour   1

Masters & Mistresses: JohnO'Dear
White Taxables: John O'Dear   1

Masters & Mistresses: John Boid
White Taxables: John Boid   1
Negro Women: Minerva   1

Masters & Mistresses:
Duncan Mackeithan
White Taxables: Duncan Mackeithan   1
Men Slaves: Abraham   1

Masters & Mistresses:
William How
White Taxables: William How   1

Masters & Mistresses:
Samuel Macree
White Taxables: Samuel Macree   1
Men Slaves: Jim, Quash & Cuffy   3

Masters & Mistresses: John Small
White Taxables: John Small   1

Masters & Mistresses:
Donald McKeithan
White Taxables: Donald McKeithan   1
Men Slaves: Quako   1
Negro Women: Cobbah   1

Masters & Mistresses:
Archibald McBride
White Taxables: Archibald McBride, Malcum McBride & Duncan McBride   3

Masters & Mistresses: John Pemberton
White Taxables: John Pemberton & James Pemberton   2
Men Slaves: Dick   1
Negro Women: Amy   1

Masters & Mistresses:
Christopher Goodwin
White Taxables: Christopher Goodwin & Peter Mc nasn[?]   2
Men Slaves: Nero & Will   2

Masters & Mistresses: Ralph Miller
White Taxables: Ralph Miller Senr. & Ralph Miller Junr   2
Men Slaves: York & Peter   2
Negro Women: Flora, Penny & Darcus   3
Boys: James   1

Masters & Mistresses: Ann Maultsby
White Taxables: John Maultsby, James Maultsby & Samuel Roots   3
Men Slaves: Scipio   1
Negro Women: Jane & Ambo   2

Masters & Mistresses:
Archibald Shaw
White Taxables: Archibald Shaw   1

Masters & Mistresses: John Campbell
White Taxables: John Campbell   1

Masters & Mistresses:
Archibald Baxter
White Taxables: Archibald Baxter   1

Masters & Mistresses:
Archibald McKeithan
White Taxables: Archibald McKeithan   1

Masters & Mistresses:
Moses Holms
White Taxables: Moses Holms & David Taylor   2

Masters & Mistresses:
James Brownlow
White Taxables: James Brownlow, T[Faded] [Faded] & [Torn]ar   3

Masters & Mistresses:
James Stuart
White Taxables: James Stuart   1
Men Slaves: Wilmore & Carlos   2
Negro Women: Philis   1

Masters & Mistresses:
Daniel McFatter
White Taxables: Daniel McFatter   1

Chapter 4: Bladen County Tax Lists of 1771

Masters & Mistresses:
Richard Small
White Taxables: Richard Small   1

Masters & Mistresses:
Richard Singletary
White Taxables: Richard Singletary & William
Singletary   2
Men Slaves: Pomp, Charles, Tom & young
Pomp   4
Negro Women   1

Masters & Mistresses:
Archibald McFatter
White Taxables: Archibald MCFatter & Daniel
McFatter   2

Masters & Mistresses:
Benoni Cleayton
White Taxables: Benoni Cleayton   1

Masters & Mistresses:
George Lyon
White Taxables: George Lyon   1

White Taxables: Archible Darrow   1
Men Slaves: Harrey   1

White Taxables: John Shaw & Gilbert Shaw   2
Men Slaves   1

White Taxables: William Forrister & Steven
Shipad[?]   2

White Taxables: Jonadab Russ   1

White Taxables: Jesse Olifent   1

Masters & Mistresses:
Elizabeth Bartram
White Taxables: Elizabeth Bartram, Wm
Bartram, Thos Baley & Jon Halsey   3
Men Slaves   11
Negro Women   6

Masters & Mistresses: Hugh Waddell Esqr.
White Taxables: Robert Barrey   2
Men Slaves   14
Negro Women   14
One pair of Char Wheels

****

BLADEN COUNTY TAX LIST OF 1771

The within list taken by me and Returned to
August Court 1771 -- John Smith

Headings in this list include: Masters or
Mistrisis, Freeman, Sons or Servants, Black
Males, Males not Sixteen, Females & Total.

Masters or Mistrisis: Stephen Anderes
Freeman: Jacob Warin
Black Males: Jack & Roger
Total   4

Masters or Mistrisis: William Howard
Black Males: Barna
Females: Rana
Total   3

Masters or Mistrisis: Daniel Melvin
Freeman: Christopher Sutton
Total   2

Masters or Mistrisis: William Saltar
Freeman: Thos. McAntoy
Sons or Servants: John & James Saltar
Black Males: Sharper, Cato, Abram, Kilbery,
Daniel, Quash, & Pomp
Males not Sixteen: Boy Jem
Females: Dido, Mary Ann, Bella & Nanny
Total   16

Masters or Mistrisis: John Hilburn
Sons or Servants: Henery Hilburn
Total   2

Masters or Mistrisis: William Register
Total   1

Masters or Mistrisis: John Sykes
Total   1

Masters or Mistrisis: Joseph Anderes
Females: Cate
Total   2

Masters or Mistrisis: Peter Broades
Black Males: William & Jupiter
Males not Sixteen: boy Prince
Females: Beersheba
Total   5

Masters or Mistrisis: Thomas Cox
Total   1

Masters or Mistrisis: William Stewart
Sons or Servants: Patrick Stewart
Black Males: Will, Lewis, Harry & Camelton
Males not Sixteen: Sterlin, Loan[?], Sam
Females: Dinah, Melah, Vilet & Phene
Total   13

Masters or Mistrisis: William Cromartie
Freeman: John Doan
Total   2

Masters or Mistrisis: [Torn] B. Beaty
Black Males: Cupit, filander, Capefear Benj.
Females: Quashabe, Eve & Eve
Total   7

Masters or Mistrisis: John Anderes
Sons or Servants: John Anderes
Black Males: free, Cato & Tony
Females: Su
Total   6

Masters or Mistrisis: Edward Reeves
Total   1

Masters or Mistrisis: Samuel Boazman
Freeman: David Mote
Total   2

Masters or Mistrisis: Joseph Howard
Freeman: Hezekiah Howard
Black Males: Tony
Total   3

Masters or Mistrisis: John Howard
Sons or Servants: William Howard
Black Males: Sharper
Males not Sixteen: Tom
Females: Hannah
Total: 5

Masters or Mistrisis: Othniel Straughan, Constable
Sons or Servants: Alexander Straughan
Black Males: Jem Quach
Females: Nan
Total: 4

Masters or Mistrisis: Beaumount Sutton
Freeman: William Sutton
Sons or Servants: Beaumount Sutton
Black Males: Holly
Total   4

Masters or Mistrisis: John Fowler
Total   1

Masters or Mistrisis: Benjamin Howard
~~Like to be on the parish~~

Masters or Mistresses: John Sutton
Total   1

Masters or Mistrisis: Nathan Meredith
Total   1

Masters or Mistrisis: David Lloyd
Freeman: Richard Lloyd
Sons or Servants: John Thomas
Black Males: York
Females: Sophia & Chloe
Total: 6

Masters or Mistrisis: James West
Total   1

Masters or Mistrisis: James West Junior
Total   1

Masters or Mistrisis: John Nickolson
Total   1

Masters or Mistrisis: Alexander Mingis Mr Gibsons Overseer
Black Males: Hary, Thuride[?] & Cesar
Females: Hannah, Florr, Nan, Amey & Florr
Total   9

Masters or Mistrisis: George Thomas Senior
Freeman: Richard Mason
Sons or Servants: David Thomas
Black Males: Providence
Total   4

Masters or Mistrisis: James Benson
Freeman: James Dowey
Total   2

Masters or Mistrisis: David Lock
Sons or Servants: David Lock
Black Males: junior Sumerset & Jo
Females: Peg
Total   5

Masters or Mistrisis: Ephraim Mulford
Freeman: John Smith
Black Males: Prince & Harry
Females: Bet & Chloe
Total   6

Masters or Mistrisis: Thomas Howard
Sons or Servants: Isaiah Howard
Total   2

Masters or Mistrisis: Benjamin Fitzrandolph
Sons or Servants: Charles Bridges
Females: Floro
Total   3

Masters or Mistrisis: Hudnal Huffane
Total   1

Masters or Mistrisis: Josiah Wilson
Black Males: Syrus & Jack
Total   3

Masters or Mistrisis: Matthew Garvan
Total   1

Masters or Mistrisis: Thomas Russ
Sons or Servants: Eleazer Russ
Black Males: Tom
Females: Bet
Total   4

Masters or Mistrisis: James Evers
Black Males: Venter
Total   2

Masters or Mistrisis: George Thomas junior
Total   1

Masters or Mistrisis: Francis Lucas
Black Males: Valentine
Males not Sixteen: Sam, Tom & Lewis
Females: Statirah & Mary
Total   7

Masters or Mistrisis: John Russ
Freeman: Charles Burk
Black Males: Pompe
Total   3

Masters or Mistrisis: William Oliphant,
Constable
Total   0

Masters or Mistrisis: Joseph Lock
Freeman: William Streete
Sons or Servants: Leonard Lock
Black Males: Tony
Females: Peg
Total   5

Masters or Mistrisis: Jacob Sykes
Total   1

Masters or Mistrisis: Thomas Suggs
Total   1

Masters or Mistrisis: Moses Ratliff
Black Males: Dick
Females: Bess, amey & Venus
Total   5

Masters or Mistrisis: Thomas Cashwell
Total   1

Masters or Mistrisis: John Cashwell
Total   1

Masters or Mistrisis: Allin McDugal
Sons or Servants: Ronnel McDugal
Total   2

Masters or Mistrisis: John Singletary
Black Males: Nap
Total   2

Masters or Mistrisis: Isaac Hays
Freeman: Samuel Freeman
Sons or Servants: John Hays
Black Males: Boson
Females: Hannah & Elizabeth
Total   6

Masters or Mistrisis: William Woolly
Sons or Servants: James Woolley
Total   2

Masters or Mistrisis: Hezekiah Davis
Females: Sarah
Total   2

Masters or Mistrisis: Edmund Crutchfield
Sons or Servants: Richard Crutchfield
Total   2

Masters or Mistrisis: Joseph Clarke Esqr
Black Males: Tom, Cesar, Johnny, Tomboy &
Jamme
Males not Sixteen: Boy Johnny
Females: Bess, Nanny, Mimbo, Hannah, Juno
& Mary
Total   13

Masters or Mistrisis: Bray Hargrove
Sons or Servants: John Hargrove
Total   2

Masters or Mistrisis: William Lewis
Total   1

CHAPTER 5

BLADEN COUNTY TAX LISTS OF 1772

BLADEN COUNTY TAX LIST OF 1772

A List of those that has not Given in their Lists

Captain Cains District 1772

A True Account of the Valuation of this District William Nevin[?]

There are no headings in this list.

Turkel McNeal
John McFarson
Godfrey McNeal
John McKay
John McFaul
John Stuart
Hector McNeal
Archibald McLochan
John McSwain
Mr McSwain
George Waker
Wm Hushens[?]

****

BLADEN COUNTY TAX LIST OF 1772

A True list of Taxables Taken in the year 1772 by me Archd. McKissak

Headings in this list include: Whites, Blacks, Mulatoes & No.

Whites: Hector McNeill Esqr., his son Alexr. & Ezekiel Smith   3
No.   3

Whites: Thomas Creel   1
No.   1

Whites: William Hubbard   1
No.   1

Whites: Thos. Brown Junr.   1
No.   1

Whites: William Taylor   1
No.   1

Whites: Demsey Bairfield   1
No.   1

Whites: John Fiveash & son Demsey   2
No.   2

Whites: Elisha Sweetin   1
Blacks: a Negro boye Do a Girl pegg   2
No.   3

Whites: Benjamin Odom, Andrew [Torn] & Demsey Tolar   3
No.   3

Whites: Charles Thompson & son William 2
No.   2

Whites: Charles Bullock   1
No.   1

Whites: Thos Townsend & son William   2
No.   2

Whites: John Cairsey & son Jacob   2
Blacks: a Negro fellow Brunswick & a wench Abb   2
Mulatoes: *William Horn*   1
No.   5

Whites: William Moore as Const. & Charles Barker   2
No.   2

Whites: Henry Bird   1
No.   1

Chapter 5:   Bladen County Tax Lists of 1772

Whites: Thos Odom, Thos. Proctor & Barnabas Lam   3
Blacks: a Negroe wench Dicy   1
No.   4

Whites: Charles Bairfield   1
No.   1

Mulatoes: *Isaac Lam & sons Nich[?] & Ephraim*   3
No.   3

Whites: John Odom & sons William & Aaron   3
No.   3

Whites: William Roazer, his father & Bro. Daniel   3
No.   3

Whites: Abram Paul   1
No.   1

Whites: John McLean   1
No.   1

Whites: William Baker   1
No.   1

Whites: John Cade   1
Blacks: Wenches Nell, Kate & a Negroe boye Jacob   3
No.   4

Whites: Jas Johnston   1
Blacks a Negroe wench anaka & a Girl Chloe   2
Mulatoes: *William Wilkins*   1
No.   4

Robt. Terrel
Blacks: his Negroe fellow Harry   1
No.   1

Whites: Adam Ivey   1
No.   1

Mulatoes: *Gilbert Cox*   1
No.   1

Whites: Cornelius Ferrel   1
No.   1

Whites: Jas. Perry   1
Mulatoes: *Simon Cox*   1
No.   2

Mulatoes: *Gutterage Lockliar*   1
No.   1

Whites: Thomas Ivey   1
No.   1

Whites: Isom Ivey   1
No.   1

Whites: Samuel Edwards   1
No.   1

Whites: Joseph Mercer   1
No.   1

Whites: John Edens & son William   2
No.   2

Whites: Chambers Humphrey   1
No.   1

Whites: Lewis Jenkins   1
No.   1

Whites: English Thomas Jackson   1
No.   1

Whites: Jacob Sellers   1
No.   1

Whites: James Trowel   1
No.   1

Whites: Archd. McLean   1
No.   1

Mulatoes: *Cannon Cumbo*   1
No.   1

Mulatoes: *Stephen Cumbo & son Jacob*   2
No.   2

Whites: Benjamin Dees   1
Mulatoes: Benjamin Sweat   1
No.   2

Mulatoes: *Edward Lockliar*   1
No.   1

Mulatoes: *Moses Turner*   1
No.   1

Whites: Alexr. McDaniel & son Benjamin 2
No. _____ 2

Whites: Edward Flowers &   sons John &
Drewry & James Turner   4
No. _____ 4

Whites: William Coward   1
No. _____ 1

Whites: Miles Bairfield   1
No. _____ 1

Whites: Shadrach Inman   1
No. _____ 1

Whites: Jesse Pittman, Joel Pittman, Thos.
Pittman & son Thos.   4
No. _____ 4

Whites: Samson Pittman   1
No. _____ 1

Whites: Joseph Milton   1
No. _____ 1

Whites: Jacob Pittman   1
No. _____ 1

Whites: Stephen Glair   1
Blacks: Negroe wench Jane   1
No. _____ 2

Whites: George Willis   1
No. _____ 1

Whites: James Wilkinson   1
No. _____ 1

Whites: Benjamin Fuller   1
Blacks: a Negroe wench patt   1
No. _____ 2

Whites: John Branch Const. & son William 2
No. _____ 2

Whites: Abram Strickland   1
No. _____ 1

Whites: John Paul   1
No. _____ 1

Mulatoes: *James Ivey & Gideon Grant*   2
No. _____ 2

Mulatoes: *Isaac Groome*   1
No. _____ 1

Mulatoes: *Joseph Ivey*   1
No. _____ 1

Whites: Edmond Brown   1
No. _____ 1

Whites: [Torn]loman Whitley   1
No. _____ 1

Mulatoes: *Peter Cairsey*   1
No. _____ 1

Whites: William Cooke   1
No. _____ 1

Whites: Solomon Mercer & son John   2
Blacks: Negro fellow Limerick   1
No. _____ 3

Whites: Ralph Riggan   1
No. _____ 1

Whites: Malachia Mercer   1
No. _____ 1

Whites: Shadrach Lee & his father Jon. Lee 2
No. _____ 2

Whites: Samuel   Andrews & sons Samuel,
Absalom & Esa   4
No. _____ 4

Whites: Joseph Rigan & son Richard   2
Blacks: a Negroe fellow Quaco & wenches
patience & Lucy   3
No. _____ 5

Whites: Abram Richardson   1
No. _____ 1

Whites: John Rigan   1
No. _____ 1

Whites: Thos. Muselwhite & sons Milbee &
Nathan   3
Blacks: a Negroe boy Henry   1
No. _____ 4

Mulatoes: *John Wilson*   1
No. _____ 1

Whites: Benjamin Freeman   1
No. _____ 1

Whites: Thos. Jackson & brother John	2
No.	2

Whites: Moses Cox	1
No.	1

Whites: Daniel Willis	1
Blacks: Negroe fellow Sam	1
No.	2

Whites: Thomas Rolin	1
No.	1

Whites: Hardy Inman & John Brown	2
No.	2

Mulatoes: *John Hammons & Wife*	2
No.	2

Mulatoes: *David Braveboye & Wife*	2
No.	2

Whites: John Smith	1
Blacks: fifteen Negroes but there name mislaid somehow so that I Can't find it Readily	
No.	16

Whites: Samuel Smith	1
Blacks: a Negroe fellow peter & wenches Dina, Doll & Cloe	4
No.	5

Whites: Nathan Horn	1
No.	1

Whites: Jas. Inman & Henry Flowers	2
No.	2

Whites: William Brumble	1
No.	1

Whites: Jacob Blunt	1
No.	1

Whites: John Blunt	1
Blacks: Negroe fellow york	1
No.	2

Whites: James Blunt	1
No.	1

Whites: Philip Blunt	1
No.	1

Whites: Joseph Bagget	1
No.	1

Whites: Jesse Harrol	1
No.	1

Whites: Elisha Harrol	1
Blacks: Negroe fellow Sam & wenches philis & Voilet	3
No.	4

Whites: William Bird	1
No.	1

Whites: Jas Rolland & sons Jas., Wm., Nathan & Saml. Rollands	5
No.	5

Whites: Lam Britt	1
No.	1

Whites: Nathaniel Richardson & brother Samuel	2
No.	2

Whites: John & Joab Baxely & William Penny[?]	3
No.	3

Whites: William Baxely	1
No.	1

Whites: Jesse Muselwhite	1
No.	1

Taxables Given me by Mary Magee	
Whites: Aaron Odom, Jacob Odom, Silas Adkins & Wm Lettarmer[?]	4
Mulatoes: *Jas. Sweat*	1
No.	5

Whites: Edmond Baxely	1
No.	1

Whites: Wm. Baxely & John Shoewesler[?]	2
No.	2

Whites: Reuben Robts.	1
Blacks: a negroe boy Cob	1
No.	2

Whites: John Sterling & Joel Wells	2
Blacks: negroe wench Bess	1
No.	3

Chapter 5:   Bladen County Tax Lists of 1772

Whites: Henry Taylor	1
No.	1

Whites: Samson Pope	1
Blacks: Negroe wench Beck & a boy Luke	2
No.	3

Whites: Henry Pope	1
Blacks: a Negroe boy Tom & a Girl Tock	2
No.	3

Whites: Jacob Pope	1
Blacks: Negroe Girl Luce	1
No.	2

Whites: Joseph Oates	1
Blacks: Negroe fellows anthony, Joe & a wench Painter	3
No.	4

Whites: Ignacious Flowers	1
No.	1

Whites: Abram Barnes Esqr.	1
Blacks: Negroe wench Sue & boy Jack	2
No.	3

Whites: [Torn]ihel Barnes	1
No.	1

Whites: Benjamin Britt Junr.	1
No.	1

Whites: Thos. Litle & son William	2
No.	2

Whites: Eliz. Best & sons John & Bryant Best	2
No.	2

Whites: William Jones	1
No.	1

Whites: Carraway Oates	1
No.	1

Whites: Edward Grantham	1
Blacks: Negroe fellow hampton	1
No.	2

Whites: William Briggs	1
No.	1

Mulatoes: *Arthur Lam*	1
No.	1

Whites: William Grantham	1
No.	1

Whites: William Studiven	1
No.	1

Whites: William Runnels	1
Blacks: Negroe fellow Jack & a wench Hanah	2
No.	3

Whites: Benjamin Ivey	1
No.	1

Whites: John Philips	1
No.	1

Whites: Zachariah Lee	1
Blacks: Negroe Wench Deborah	1
No.	2

Whites: William Ferrol	1
No.	1

Mulatoes: *Jas. Carter & sons Isaac & Jas. Carter*	3
No.	3

Whites: Ben Tomas	1
Mulatoes: *Solomon Jas. & son Solomon*	2
No.	3

Whites: Jacob Alford	1
No.	1

Whites: Thos. Talton Junr. & James & Thos. Talton	3
No.	3

Mulatoes: *Thos. Cairsey*	1
No.	1

Whites: Hugh Brown & sons Neil & William Brown	3
Blacks: Negroe Wench Sarah	1
No.	4

Whites: Jas. Moore & son John	2
No.	2

Whites: David Bairfield	1
No.	1

Whites: Nathan Britt	1
No.	1

Whites: Thos. Smith & John	2	
No.	2	

Whites: William Tolar as Const. & Isaac Quarting	2	
No.	2	

Whites: William Wilkinson & son Wm.	2	
No.	2	

Mulatoes: *Aaron Drake*	1	
No.	1	

Whites: Jesee Glas	1	
No.	1	

Whites: Levi Ennis	1	
No.	1	

Whites: John Gibson	1	
Blacks: Negroe fellow Cailis & wenches pleasant & Lucy	3	
No.	4	

Whites: John Britt	1	
No.	1	

Whites: Jonathan Taylor as Const	1	
No.	1	

Whites: Benjamin Britt & son Jesee	2	
No.	2	

Whites: Thos. Low	1	
No.	1	

Whites: John Bullard Senr	1	
No.	1	

Whites: Benjamin Lam	1	
No.	1	

Whites: William Butlar	1	
No.	1	

Mulatoes: *Edmond Revel & Wife*	2	
No.	2	

Mulatoes: *Ishmael Cheves*	1	
No.	1	

Mulatoes: *John Lockeliar & Wife & son Robert*	3	
No.	3	

Mulatoes: *William Lockeliar*	1	
No.	1	

Mulatoes: *Jacob Lockeliar*	1	
No.	1	

Whites: Thos. Bullard	1	
No.	1	

Whites: Ambrous Bullard	1	
No.	1	

Whites: Thos. Sterling	1	
No.	1	

Whites: James Risen	1	
No.	1	

Whites: Henry Smith	1	
No.	1	

Whites: John Bues	1	
No.	1	

Whites: Tarlor ogwin & son John	2	
No.	2	

Whites: Hardy ogwin	1	
No.	1	

Whites: Tarlor ogwin Junr	1	
No.	1	

Whites: Daniel McLean	1	
Blacks: a Negroe boye [Torn]	1	
No.	2	

Whites: Thomas Cairsey Senr.	1	
Blacks: Negroe fellows Dick & Quac[?]	2	
No.	3	

Whites: William Freeman	1	
No.	1	

Mulatoes: *William Sweat & son George*	2	
No.	2	

Whites: Richd. Grantham	1	
No.	1	

Whites: William Capps	1	
No.	1	

Whites: Charles Jordon & son Matthew	2	
No.	2	

Whites: John Jordon	1
No.	1

Whites: Joseph Jordon	1
No.	1

Whites: Lazarus Creal	1
No.	1

Whites: Jonathan Taylor as Const.	1
No.	1

Whites: Joseph Strikland	1
No.	1

Whites: Richd. Smith	1
Blacks: Negroe fellow Robin & a wench Cloe	2
No.	3

Whites: Thos. Russell	1
No.	1

Whites: Noah Mercer	1
No.	1

Mulatoes: *John Cumbo*	1
No.	1

****

BLADEN COUNTY TAX LIST OF 1772

John Grange Esqr List for the Year 1772

Headings for this list include: Whites, Molatoes, Black Males, Black Females, Boys, Carrage Wheels & Total.

Whites: Charles Benbow	4
Black Males	1
Black Females	1
Total	6

Whites: John Campbell	1
Molatoes	20
Black Males	18
Black Females	4
Total	43

Whites: Daniel Currey	1
Total	1

Whites: Thomas Chiles	1
Molatoes	8
Black Males	6
Total	15

Whites: Marmaduke Jones	2
Black Males	18
Black Females	13
Boys	1
Carrage Wheels	2
Total	34

Whites: John Jones	1
Black Males	1
Black Females	3
Total	5

Whites: Berringer Moore	1
Black Males	4
Black Females	6
Boys	2
Total	13

Whites: Thomas McGuire	2
Black Males	15
Black Females	18
Boys	3
Carrage Wheels	6
Total	38

Whites: Mary Newton	0
Molatoes	5
Black Males	2
Total	7

Whites: John Smith	1
Total	1

Whites: Aron Vardee	1
Total	1

****

BLADEN COUNTY TAX LIST OF 1772

Peter Lord Esqr List of Taxables for the Year 1772

Headings in this list include: Whites, Free Negros & Mulatoes, Male Slaves, Female Slaves, Slaves Under Sixteen, Chair Wheels & Total.

Whites: Thomas Adkeson	1
Total	1

Whites: Oxford and James Beasley	2
Total	2

Whites: John Boherd & John Dormon	2
Total	2

Whites: Duncan Boiy [Bory?]	1
Total	1

Whites: Samuel Beltman	1
Total	1

Whites: John Beuey	1
Total	1

Whites: Bastain Barnes	1
Total	1

Whites: Samuel & stephen Butler	2
Male Slaves	4
Female Slaves	1
Total	7

Whites: Duncan & Hugh Campbell	2
Male Slaves	1
Total	3

Whites: Joseph & Benja. Cooper	2
Male Slaves	2
Total	4

Whites: Peter Carpenter	1
Total	1

Whites: Abel Corbet	1
Total	1

Whites: Samuel Canneday & son Jacob	2
Male Slaves	1
Female Slaves	1
Total	4

Whites: Samuel Canneday Junr.	1
Total	1

Whites: Cy[Faded]	1
Total	1

Whites: William Donoho & William Collins	
	2
Total	2

Whites: Drury Morgan	1
Total	1

Whites: Richard Elwell	1
Male Slaves	1
Slaves Under Sixteen	1
Total	3

Whites: James Ellis and Thomas Moore	2
Male Slaves	3
Female Slaves	1
Slaves Under Sixteen	2
Total	8

[The rest of the above list is missing.]

****

BLADEN COUNTY TAX LIST OF 1772

David Morlow Esqr List of Taxables for the Year 1772

Headings in this list include: Whites, Free Negroes & Mulatoes, Male Slaves, Female Slaves, Boys Under Sixteen, Carrage Wheels & Total.

Whites: Joseph Adams	1
Total	1

Whites: Henry Bozwell	1
Total	1

Whites: Thomas Broder	1
Total	1

Whites: John Busby & two Sons	3
Total	3

Whites: Miles Busby	2
Total	1

Whites: John Bauldwin	1
Male Slaves	2
Total	3

Whites: Thomas Brown & Sons	4
Total	4

Whites: James Brown	1
Total	1

Whites: John Butler	1
Total	1

Chapter 5:   Bladen County Tax Lists of 1772

Whites: Luke Barefield	1
Male Slaves	2
Female Slaves	3
Total	6

Whites: William Brown	1
Total	1

Whites: John Branton	1
Total	1

Whites: John Clark	1
Male Slaves	1
Female Slaves	1
Total	3

Whites: John Carlile	1
Total	1

Whites: Moses Coleman	1
Total	1

Whites: George Clark	1
Total	1

Whites: David Dunken	2
Male Slaves	2
Total	4

Whites: George Duke	1
Total	1

Whites: Abram Danford	1
Total	1

Whites: Thomas Dyson & Jack [or Josh] Walters	2
Total	2

Whites: Daniel Fling	1
Total	1

Whites: John Gilliard	1
Male Slaves	1
Total	2

Whites: Caleb Galaway	1
Total	1

Whites: Ezekiel Hill	3
Total	3

Whites: William Horn	1
Male Slaves	1
Total	2

Whites: Southey Hays	1
Total	1

Whites: Thomas Hays	1
Total	1

Whites: Thomas Hardwick & 2 Sons	3
Total	3

Whites: Belitha Hays	2
Total	2

Whites: Jacob Hanchee	1
Total	1

[The rest of the above list is missing.]

****

BLADEN COUNTY TAX LIST OF 1772

This List taken for ye year 1772

Headings for this list include: White Men, Black Fellows, Women, Boys & Girls & Total.

White Men: Edwd. Bryan	1
Black Fellows	1
Total	2

White Men: Saml Evers	1
Total	1

White Men: Benjm. Humphrey ~~Jos. Humphrey & James White~~	1
Total	1

White Men: George Brown & Jos [Jon?] his Son	2
Women	2
Boys & Girls	2
Total	6

White Men: Stephen Brown	1
Total	1

White Men: Wm Olifent overseer of Brumpton[?] Neagroes	1
Black Fellows	11
Women	6
Boys & Girls	3
Total	20

Chapter 5: Bladen County Tax Lists of 1772

White Men: Samuel McRee	1
Black Fellows	3
Total	4

White Men: Robt. McConkey & Wm Bridges	2
Black Fellows	1
Women	1
Total	4

White Men: John Hill	1
Total	1

White Men: John McGlachlain	1
Total	1

White Men: Dennis Lennon & Peter Carpenter	2
Black Fellows	1
Total	3

White Men: John Roberts	1
Total	1

White Men: John Dryden	1
Total	1

White Men: David Bryan	1
Total	1

White Men: John Bryan & Thos Moris	2
Women	1
Total	3

White Men: Elizabeth Harrison her son Edwd	1
Black Fellows	1
Women	1
Boys & Girls	1
Total	4

White Men: Philemon Bryan and son Philemon	2
Women	1
Total	3

White Men: Jacob Muns	1
Total	1

White Men: Stephen Hester	1
Total	1

White Men: John Adair	1
Total	1

White Men: [Torn], John White[?] & Joseph Humphrey	3
Total	3

White Men: Amey Bryan	0
Black Fellows	1
Women	2
Total	

White Men: John Bentley	1
Total	1

White Men: Samuel Currey & Wm Dowlas	2
Total	2

White Men: Wm Singletary & Saml Porter	2
Black Fellows	1
Women	1
Total	4

White Men: Edwd Davis	1
Women	1
Total	2

White Men: David White, David Owen & James Ervin	3
Black Fellows	2
Total	4

White Men: Saml. Gyton	1
Total	1

White Men: Wm Russ & Edmond Russ	2
Total	2

White Men: Wm. Smith	1
Total	1

White Men: Wm Handen & Wm Handen Junr.	2
Black Fellows	1
Women	1
Total	4

White Men: John Russ and son John	2
Total	2

White Men: David Russ	1
Total	1

White Men: James Baley, Duncan Morison & James Smith	3
Black Fellows	6
Women	2
Total	11

Chapter 5:   Bladen County Tax Lists of 1772

White Men: Thos. Hestors & John Hestors 2
Total _____ 2

White Men: Jesse Howard _____ 1
Total _____ 1

White Men: Charils Dent Constable _____

The above list taken Pr Wm. McRee

****

BLADEN COUNTY TAX LIST OF 1772

John Turner Esqr List of Taxables for the
Year 1772

Headings for this list include: Whites, Free
Negroes & Mulatoes, Male Slaves, Female
Slaves, Slaves Under Sixteen, Carriage Wheels
& Total.

Whites: Benjamin Arrington _____ 1
Female Slaves _____ 1

Whites: Stephen Briton Coln. Dry[?] Overseer
_____ 1
Male Slaves _____ 16
Female Slaves _____ 9
Slaves Under Sixteen _____ 1
Total _____ 27

Whites: Dugal Bl[?]as _____ 1
Total _____ 1

Whites: John and Charles Bauldwin __ 2
Male Slaves: _____ 3
Female Slaves _____ 2
Slaves Under Sixteen _____ 1
Total _____ 8

Whites: William Bryan _____ 1
Male Slaves _____ 1
Total _____ 2

Whites: Morris [Moses] Buie[?] & Thos. Jones
_____ 2
Total _____ 2

Whites: Ezekiel Busbey _____ 1
Total _____ 1

Whites: William Burney _____ 1
Total _____ 1

Whites: William Boyte & Gabriel Parker 2
Total _____ 2

Whites: Simon & Richard Brite _____ 2
Total _____ 2

Whites: Jeremiah Bigford Senr. & son Jeremiah
_____ 2
Female Slaves _____ 1

Whites: James & Joseph Bauldwin ___ 2
Male Slaves _____ 1
Female Slaves _____ 1
Total _____ 4

Whites: Benjamin Busby[?] _____ 1
Total _____ 1

Whites: John Brother _____ 1
Total _____ 1

Whites: William Barefoot _____ 1
Male Slaves _____ 1
[Torn] _____

Whites: George & [Torn] Ba[?] [Torn] _____

Whites: William Burney
[Torn] [Torn] _____

****

BLADEN COUNTY TAX LIST OF 1772

North Carolina Bladen County A True List of
all the Taxable Persons Taking in By Isaac
Ray and to be Returned To the Inferior Coart
held in August For the Yeare One Thousand
Seven hundred and Seventy two

Headings for this list include: Whites, Blacks
& No.

Whites: John Anderson _____ 1
No. _____ 1

Whites: William Anderson _____ 1
No. _____ 1

Whites: John Averay _____ 2
No. _____ 2

Whites: James Beard _____ 3
Blacks _____ 1
No. _____ 4

87

Whites: Larrance Byrne		5
No.		5
Whites: Thos. Bedsole		1
No.		1
Whites: James Bennett		1
No.		1
Whites: Joseph Butler		1
Blacks		3
No.		4
Whites: Dannell Bearde		1
No.		1
Whites: John Bearde		1
Blacks		1
No.		2
Whites: Samuel Caine		2
Blacks		1
No.		3
Whites: Benjeamin Clark		2
No.		2
Whites: John Cashwell		1
No.		1
Whites: Joseph Carter		2
No.		2
Whites: Jessey Carter		1
No.		1
Whites: Henrey Clarke		1
No.		1
Whites: William Caine		3
No.		3
Whites: Benjeamin Clarke		1
Blacks		3
No.		4
Whites: Cade Weatherbee		2
Blacks		1
No.		3
Whites: John Davis		1
No.		1
Whites: Beaxster Davees		1
No.		1

Whites: John Edmenson		1
Blacks		1
No.		2
Whites: John Elwell		1
Blacks		1
No.		2
Whites: Mikell Euestres		1
No.		1
Whites: Stephen Freeman		1
No.		1
Whites: John Fearris[?]		1
No.		1
Whites: John Green		1
Blacks		1
No.		2
Whites: John Gervices		1
No.		1
Whites: Robart Grice		1
No.		1
Whites: [Faded] Jasub		1
No.		1
Whites: [Faded] Goardon		2
No.		2
Whites: [Faded] Hoalten		1
[Faded]		
White: [Faded]hue Higgones		2
Blacks		1
No.		3
Whites: [Faded] Hollensworth		1
No.		1
Whites: Stephen Hollenworth		2
No.		2
Whites: Nathaniel Reaves		2
Blacks		2
No.		4
Whites: Thos. Lock		1
Blacks		1
No.		2

Whites: David Miles	1
No.	1

Whites: William McMaster	2
No.	2

Whites: David McDonnell	1
No.	1

Whites: Archable McDonnell	1
No.	1

Whites: James Donnell	2
Blacks	3
No.	5

Whites: John Bartin [?] will	2
Blacks	1
No.	3

Whites: Eli & Even Plummer	2
No.	2

Whites: Gidion Prickett	1
No.	1

Whites: Jeremiah Plummer	1
No.	1

Whites: Robart Richardson	1
No.	1

Whites: Joseph Ray	1
No.	1

Whites: John Richardson Junr.	3
No.	3

Whites: Thos. Richardson	1
No.	1

Whites: Moses Ratleff	1
Blacks	3
No.	4

Whites: Samual Sutten	2
No.	2

Whites: Elizabeth Singletary	3
Blacks	4
No.	7

Whites: [?] Sargoner	2
Blacks	4
No.	6

Whites: Richard Singletary	2
Blacks	1
No.	3

Whites: John Suggs	1
No.	1

Whites: Thomas Suggs	1
No.	1

Whites: Thomas Sessomes	2
No.	2

Whites: John Smith	1
No.	1

Whites: James West	1
No.	1

Whites: William Wilkenson	2
No.	2

Whites: William Bretford	1
No.	1

Whites: James Singletary	0
Blacks	1
No.	1

Whites: John Harrison Jur.	2
No.	2

Whites: Andrew Graham	1
No.	1

John Johnston And Wife	
Whites	1
Blacks	1
No.	2
[This entry indicates that one of the individuals above is a person of color]	

Whites: William Jonston	3
No.	3

Whites: Josiah Jonston	1
No.	1

Whites: Richard Hammones	1
No.	1

Whites: Titus Overturn	1
No.	1

Whites: [Faded] Edwards 1
No. 1

[Extra Names at bottom of page.]

James West	1 tax
Mary Storm	1 Tax
Solomon Wilson	1 Tax
John Parnell	1 Tax

****

BLADEN COUNTY TAX LIST OF 1772

John Smith Esqr List of Taxables for the Year 1772

Headings in this list include: Whites, Free Mulatoes & Negroes, Male Slaves, Female Slaves, Slaves Under Sixteen, Chair Wheels & Total.

Whites: Stephen Andrews & Jacob Warren 2
Male Slaves 2
Total 4

Whites: Joseph Andrews 1
Female Slaves 1
Total 2

Whites: John Andrews and Son John 2
Male Slaves 3
Female Slaves 1
Total 6

Whites: Whites 0
Bridget Bat[?]y
Male Slaves 4
Female Slaves 3
Total 7

Whites: Peter Broadas 1
Male Slaves 2
Female Slaves 1
Slaves Under Sixteen 1
Total 5

Whites: Samuel Bozman and David Moot 2
Total 2

Whites: James Benson and James Dowey 2
Total 2

Whites: Thomas Cox 1
Total 1

Whites: William Crommerty and John Doane 2
Total 2

Whites: Thomas Cashwell 1
Total 1

Whites: John Cashwell 1
Total 1

Whites: Edmund and Richard Cruthfield 2
Total 2

Whites: Joseph Clarke 1
Male Slaves 5
Female Slaves 6
Slaves Under Sixteen 1
Total 13

Whites: Hezekiah Davis 1
Slaves Under Sixteen 1
Total 2

Whites: [Faded] [Faded] 1
Total 1

Whites: John Fowler 1
Total 1

Whites: Benja. Fitzrandolph & Chas. Bridges 2
Female Slaves 1
Total 3

Whites: Matthew Gurvon 1
Total 1

Whites: William Howard 1
Male Slaves 1
Female Slaves 1
Total 3

Whites: John and Henry Hilburn 2
Total 2

Whites: Joseph and Hezekiah Howard 2
Male Slaves 1
Total 3

Whites: John and William Howard 2
Male Slaves 1
Female Slaves 1
Slaves Under Sixteen 1
Total 5

Whites: Thomas and Jonah Howard   2
Total   2

Whites: Hudnal Huffam   1
Total   1

Whites: Isaac Hays, Saml. Freeman & John
Hays   3
Male Slaves   1
Female Slaves   2
Total   6

Whites: Bray & John Hargrove   2
Total   2

Whites: David Loyd, Richard Loyd & John
Thomas   3
Male Slaves   1
Female Slaves   2
Total   6

Whites: David Lock & son   2
Male Slaves   2
Female Slaves   1
Total   5

Whites: Francis Lucas   1
Male Slaves   1
Female Slaves   2
Slaves Under Sixteen   3
Total   7

Whites: Joseph & Lenord Lock and Wm.
Stark[?]   3
Male Slaves   1
Female Slaves   1
Total   5

Whites: William Lewis   1
Total   1

Whites: Daniel Melven & Christopher Sutton
                                     2
Total   2

Whites: Nathan Meredith   1
Total   1

Whites: Alexander Menges Mr Gibsons
Overseer   1
Male Slaves   3
Female Slaves   5
Total   9

Whites: Alen McDougald & son Ronel   2
Total   2

Whites: Ophri[?] Mulford & John Smith   2
Male Slaves   2
Female Slaves   2
Total   6

[The rest of the above list is missing.]

****

BLADEN COUNTY TAX LIST OF 1772

Joseph Clark Esqr List of 1772

Headings   in   this   list   include: Whites,
Mulatoes, Black Males, Black Females, Boys,
Chair Wheels & Total.

Whites: John Adear   1
Total   1

Whites: John Boyd   1
Black Females   1
Total   2

Whites: Archabald Baxter   1
Total   1

Whites: James Brownlow, Thos. Lennon & R.
Ven[?]   3
Total   3

Whites: Wm. Bartram, Thos. Bailey & Jno
[?]atsey   3
Black Males   11
Black Females   6
Total   20

Whites: John Campbell   1
Total   1

Whites: Benoni Clayton   1
Total   1

Whites: William Davis   1
Total   1

Whites: Archabald Darah   1
Black Males   1
Total   2

Whites: William Forrester   1
Total   1

Chapter 5:   Bladen County Tax Lists of 1772

Whites: Christopher Gooden & Peter McNam[?]
                                                2
Black Males   2
Total   4

Whites: William How   1
Total   1

Whites: Moses Homes and Daniel Taylor   2
Total   2

Whites: John Lucas, John Lucas Jur. & Jas
Carver   3
Black Males   6
Black Females   5
Boys   2
Total   16

Whites: George Lyon   1
Total   1

Whites: Daniel McFater   1
Total   1

Whites: Archabald & Daniel McFater   2
Total   2

Whites: Jacob Messick Senr. & Jacob Messick
                                                2
Total   2

Whites: Iver McKay   1
Black Males   1
Black Females   1
Total   5

Whites: Duncan McKeithan   1
Black Males   1
Total   2

Whites: Samuel McRee   1
Black Males   3
Total   4

Whites: Daniel McKeithan   1
Black Males   1
Black Females   1
Total   3

Whites: Archabald, Malcom & Duncan McBride
                                                3
Total   3

Whites: Ralph Miller Senr. & Junr.   2
Black Males   2
Black Females   3
Boys   1
Total   8

Whites: Ann Maltsby & Sons John & James &
Saml Roots[?]   3
Black Males   1
Black Females   2
Total   6

Whites: Archabald McKeithan   1
Total   1

Whites: Jesse Oliphant   1
Total   1

Whites: John Pointer & Sons John & Asgalus &
R. Mullington   4
Black Males   2
Black Females   1
Total   7

Whites: John & James Pemberton   2
Black Males   1
Black Females   1
Total   4

Whites Jonadab Russ   1
Total   1

Whites: William Smith & sons John & William
                                                3
Black Males   2
Total   5

Whites: Sarah Sumor [Seemor] & son Thomas
                                                1
Total   1

Whites: John Small   1
Total   1

Whites: Archabald Shaw   1
Total   1

Whites: James Stewart   1
Black Males   2
Black Females   1
Total   4

Whites: Richard Small   1
Total   1

Chapter 5:   Bladen County Tax Lists of 1772

Whites: Richard & Wm Singletary	2
Black Males	4
Black Females	1
Total	7

Whites: John & Gilbert Shaw	2
Total	2

Whites: Stephen Shepherd	1
Total	1

Whites: Hugh Waddell & Robert Barrey	2
Black Males	14
Black Females	14
Chair Wheels	2
Total	30

****

BLADEN COUNTY TAX LIST OF 1772

Abram Barnes Esqr List of Taxables for the Year 1772

Headings for this list include: Whites, Free Negroes & Mulatoes, Male Slaves, Female Slaves, Under Sixteen, Chair Wheels & Total.

Whites: Samuel Andrews & Sons Absalom & Samuel	3
Total	3

Whites: James Ard & sons Thomas, James & Ruben	4
Male Slaves	1
Female Slaves	2
Under Sixteen	1
Total	8

Whites: William Ard	1
Total	1

Whites: Charles Bullock	1
Total	1

Whites: William Baker	1
Total	1

Whites: Thomas Bennett	1
Total	1

Whites: Benj. Britt Junr.	1
Total	1

Whites: Lamuel Britt	1
Total	1

Whites: Henry Bird & Son William	2
Total	2

Whites: Nathan Brit	1
Total	1

Whites: David Barefield & Charles Brouder	
	2
Total	2

Whites: William Baxley	1
Total	1

Whites: James Blunt Senr. & son Reddin	2
Total	2

Whites: John Blunt & Edmund Baxley	2
Male Slaves	1
Total	3

Whites: James Blunt Junr	1
Total	1

Whites: Joseph Bagget	1
Total	1

Whites: Green Bodiford	1
Total	1

Whites: John Bullard	1
Total	1

Whites: Michael Barnes	1
Total	1

Whites: William Brumbell	1
Total	1

Free Negroes & Mulatoes: *David Braveboy & Wife*	2
Total	2

Whites: Jacob [Torn]	1
Total	1

Whites: Edward Burten [Bunten]	1
Total	1

Whites: Philip Blunt	1
Total	1

Whites: John Baxley	1
Total	1

Whites: Benja. Britt Senr. And Son Jesse   2
Total   2

Whites: Thomas Cairsey   1
Male Slaves   1
Total   2

Free Negroes & Mulatoes:
Peter Cairsey and son David   2
Total   2

Free Negroes & Mulatoes:
Joseph Clark   1
Total   1

Whites: James Craft   1
Total   1

Whites: Thomas Creel   1
Total   1

Whites: Lazerous Creel Constable   0
Total   0

Whites: Gilbert Cox & James Purcey   2
Total   2

Whites: William Coward   1
Total   1

Whites: Simon Cox   1
Total   1

Whites: James Carter & Sons James & Isaac
                                             3
Total   3

Whites: Isaac Cannady and Archabald Boon
                                             2
Total   2

Whites: John Edon   1
Total   1

Whites: Samuel Edwards   1
Total   1

Whites: Joseph Fort and James Stewart   2
Male Slaves   2
Female Slaves   3
Total   7

Whites: Benjamin Freeman   1
Total   1

Whites: William Furman   1
Total   1

Whites: Edward Flowers & sons John & David[?] & Wm Barret   4
[Torn]

[The rest of the above list is missing.]

****

BLADEN COUNTY TAX LIST OF 1772

Archabald McKessak Esqr List of Taxables for the Year 1772

Headings for this list include: Whites, Free Negroes & Mulatoes, Male Slaves, Female Slaves, Chair Wheels & Total.

Whites: Jacob Alford   1
Total   1

Whites: Hugh Brown   1
Female Slaves   1
Total   2

Whites: Edward and Thr[?]by Brown   2
Total   2

Whites: William Butler   1
Total   1

Whites: Thomas Bullard   1
Total   1

Whites: Ambrous Bullard   1
Total   1

Whites: Thomas Bryan   1
Total   1

Whites: Elizabeth Best & sons John & Bryan
                                             2
Total   2

Whites: Malcom Buye   1
Male Slaves   1
Total   2

Whites: Dempsey Barefield   1
Total   1

Whites: John Bues   1
Total   1

Whites: John Branch   1
Total   1

Whites: Briton Branch   1
Total   1

Whites: Thomas Bird   1
Total   1

Whites: Abram Barnes Esqr   1
Male Slaves   1
Female Slaves   1
Total   3

Whites: Thomas Brown Senr & Son Thomas
                                            2
Female Slaves   1
Total   3

Whites: Charles Barefield   1
Total   1

Whites: Shadrack Baget   1
Total   1

Whites: George Colley[?] and Joshua Harp 2
Total   2

Free Negroes & Mulatoes:
Ishmael Cheves   1
Total   1

Whites: Malcom Campbell   1
Total   1

Free Negroes & Mulatoes:
Cannon Cumbo   1
Total   1

Whites: Moses Cox   1
Total   1

Whites: John Cade   1
Total   1

Free Negroes & Mulatoes:
John Cairsey & Son & Wm. Horn   3
Female Slaves   1
Total   4

Free Negroes & Mulatoes:
Thomas Cairsey Junr   1
Total   1

Whites: John Dunkan   1
Total   1

Free Negroes & Mulatoes:
James Doyal and Wife   2
Total   2

Whites: James Ferquarson   1
Total   1

Whites: John Fiveash & son Dempsey   2
Total   2

Whites: Benjaman Fuller   1
Female Slaves   1
Total   2

Whites: Ignatious Flowers   1
Total   1

Whites: William & John Grantham   2
Total   2

Whites: Edward Grantham   1
Male Slaves   1
Total   2

Whites: Moses and Robert Grice   2
Total   2

Whites: William Gulledge Constable   1
Total   1

Free Negroes & Mulatoes:
Thomas Groom   1
Total   1

Whites: John Gibson   1
Male Slaves   1
Female Slaves   2
[Torn] [Torn]

Free Negroes & Mulatoes:
Frederick Goin and Wife   2
[Torn] [Torn]

[The rest of this list is missing.]

CHAPTER 6

BLADEN COUNTY TAX LISTS OF 1774

BLADEN COUNTY TAX LIST OF 1774

A List of Taxables taken by the subscriber for year 1774 from Thomas Bryan to swap Down the East side of Drowning To the Province Line on west side of White and Brown March As high as John McKown George Brown

List of Taxables Returned to George Brown Esquire August Term 1774

Headings in this list include: White Males, Negroe Males, Wenches & Total.

Whites Males : Faithfull Graham & Duncan Morrison	2
Negroe Males: Scipio & Joe	2
Wenches: Betty & Sue	2
Total	6

White Males: Simon Bright & Richard Bright	2
Total	2

White Males: James Brown	1
Total	1

White Males: Daniel McCullom	1
Total	1

White Males: Duncan Henderson	1
Total	1

White Males: Thomas[?]	1
Wenches: Peg, Gena & Marto	3
Total	4

White Males: Benjamin Arrinton	1
Wenches: Goin a Wench	1
Total	2

White Males: William Boss	1
Total	1

White Males: John McKown, Robert McKown & William McKown	3
Total	3

White Males: Joshua Hays & Isom Wiggins	2
Total	2

White Males: Solomon Lewis	1
Total	1

White Males: Ezekiel Buzby	1
Total	1

White Males: William Buzby	1
Total	1

White Males: Dennis Lennon	1
Negroe Males: Samson	1
Total	2

White Males: Charles Raborn	1
Total	1

White Males: John Raborn	1
Total	1

White Males: Joseph Powers & Charles Browder	2
Total	2

White Males: James Lewis Senr., James Lewis Junr. & Charles Dayley Criple	3
Total	3

White Males: Jerimiah Bigford & William Bigford	2
Wenches: Affy & Jude	2
Total	4

White Males: Josiah Lewis Senr. & Josiah Lewis Junr	2
Negroe Males: London	1
Wenches: Mol	1
Total	4

White Males: John Simson	1
Total	1

White Males: William McNeil & John McClarin	2
Negroe Males: Duncan & Marc	2
Wenches: Cloe & Venus	2
Total	6

White Males: Matthew Kelly	1
Negroe Males: Limbrick, Will & Jack	3
Wenches: Jude & Sall	2
Total	6

White Males: Daniel Mathis	1
Total	1

White Males: Even McMillin & Dugal McMillin	2
Total	2

White Males: William Bryant, John Bryant & William Bryant	3
Wenches: Moll	1
Total	4

White Males: Robert Walker & John Purkepine	2
Total	2

White Males: Frances Lawson & John Kersey	2
Total	2

White Males: James Shipman, Daniel Shipman	2
Negroe Males: Sam	1
Total	3

White Males: Anguish Sellers, [Faded] Sellers & Anguish Sellers	1 3
Total	3

White Males: Daniel Turnner	1
Total	1

White Males: Barnabas Stevens & Abraham Stevens	2
Negroe Males: Aro, Aberdee & Tom	3
Wenches: Dianner	1
Total	6

White Males: Joshua Stevens & Oliver Stevens	2
Negroe Males: Peter & Sam	2
Wenches: finder	1
Total	5

White Males: William Strickling & Philip Strickling	2
Total	2

White Males: Daniel McNickols & Thomas Roberson	2
Total	2

White Males: Thomas Hardick	1
Total	1

White Males: Aaron Tomlenson & Abram	2
Total	2

White Males: Thomas Browder	1
Total	1

White Males: Christopher Sanders & Daniel Shipman	2
Negroe Males: Sesar	1
Total	3

White Males: William Johnson & John Johnson	2
Total	2

White Males: John Baldwin	1
Negroe Males: Quash	1
Wenches: Beck	1
Total	3

White Males: Edward Wall	1
Total	1

White Males: John Devesters	1
Total	1

White Males: William Brown	1
Total	1

White Males: Edward Wilson	1
Total	1

White Males: John Branton, John Branton Junr & Samuel Branton	3
Total	3

White Males: Abraham King	1
Total	1

White Males: James Wilson	1
Total	1

White Males: John Coleman Constable	1
Total	1

White Males: William Horn, Inue[?] Horn & Joab Horn	3
Total	3

White Males: Moses Coleman	1
Total	1

White Males: Dinnis Dosson	1
Negroe Males: Lewis	1
Wenches: Sall	1
Total	3

White Males: John Butler	1
Total	1

White Males: Coleman Nickes	1
Negroe Males: Frank & Jacob	2
Wenches: Jenna	1
Total	4

White Males: John Roger & Jenkens Warters	2
Total	2

White Males: Thomas Bryant	
Negroe Males: Joy	1
Wenches: Grace	1
Total	2

White Males: Luke Barefield & Stephen Barefield	2
Negroe Males: Nan[?]	1
Wenches: Venus, Lucee, Nancy, Easter, Penny & Gena	6
Total	9

White Males: Thomas Dison	1
Total	1

White Males: William Boyets & Jacob Boyets	2
Total	2

White Males: Solomon Dison	1
Total	1

White Males: Belitha Hays, Sothey Hays & William Sibbets	3
Negroe Males: London	1
Total	4

White Males: Joseph Noble	1
Total	1

White Males: Nehemiah Johnson & Jacob Johnson	
[No taxables given]	

White Males: David Clark	1
Total	1

White Males: John Yates	1
Total	1

White Males: Jacob Hanchey	1
Total	1

White Males: Willis Stedephant	1
Total	1

White Males: Thomas Amis & Isaac Haris	2
Negroe Males: Joe, Peter, Joe Cowper, York, Red, Gloucester, London & Catoe	8
Wenches: Nan & Venus	2
Total	12

White Males: Ezekiel Hill & Joab Hill	2
Total	2

White Males: Thomas Hays	1
Total	1

White Males: James Money, Benjamin Money & John Money	3
Total	3

White Males: Alexander Woodsides	1
Negroe Males: Pompey	1
Wenches: Peny	1
Total	3

Amelea Marley	
Negroe Males: Will & Cudjo	2
Wenches: Darah	1
Total	3

White Males: Israel Tomlinson	1
Total	1

White Males: Thomas Johnson	1
Total	1

White Males: David Duncan	1
Negroe Males: Joe	1
Wenches: Sara	1
Total	3

White Males: John Johnson Senr.	1
Total	1

White Males: Elias Duncan	1
Total	1

Elizabeth McKay	
White Males: Simon Sellers	1
Total	1

White Males: Matthew Sellers	1
Total	1

White Males: Daniel Flin	1
Total	1

White Males: Thomas Harwick Senr. & Allen Harwick	2
Total	2

White Males: John Wilson	1
Total	1

White Males: Thos. Sanders Senr, William Sanders & Thos. Sanders Junr.	3
Negroe Males: Munday	1
Wenches: Mary	1
Total	5

White Males: Caleb Calloway & Zachariah Dyson	2
Total	2

****

BLADEN COUNTY TAX LIST OF 1774

A LIST of the Taxable Persons in Bladen County for the Year 1774

Headings for this list include: Whites, Men Slaves, Female Slaves, Boys & Total.

[This list appears to be a consolidated for the whole county.]

Wm. Singletary 2 Mix Blood Free	

Aaron Strickland 2 Whites	

Stephen Glain enter in the B's by Mistake	

Whites: John Adair	1
Total	1

Whites: Samuel Andrews	5
Total	5

Whites: Stephen Andrews	1
Men Slaves	3
Female Slaves	1
Total	5

Whites: John Andrews	3
Men Slaves	5
Female Slaves	1
Total	9

Whites: Joseph Andrews	1
Total	1

Whites: Thomas Ard	2
Men Slaves	1
Female Slaves	1
Total	4

Whites: Thomas Amis	2
Men Slaves	8
Female Slaves	2
Total	12

Whites: Benjamin Arrinton	1
Female Slaves	1
Total	2

Whites: Thomas Averett	1
Total	1

Whites: Benjamin Atkins	3
Total	3

Whites: William Anderson	1
Total	1

Whites: John Anderson	1
Total	1

Whites: James Ard	1
Boys	1
Total	2

Whites: Ruben Ard	1
Female Slaves	1
Total	2

Whites: William Ard	1
Female Slaves	1
Total	2

Whites: Thomas Atkison	1
Total	1

Whites: Silas Atkins	1
Total	1

Chapter 6:   Bladen County Tax Lists of 1774

Whites: Jacob Alford   1
Boys   1
Total   2

Whites: Simon Burney   2
Total   2

Whites: John Bentley   1
Total   1

Whites: Philemon Bryan   3
Total   3

Whites: George Brown   2
Female Slaves   2
Boys   3
Total

Whites: Robert Berry   2
Total   2

Whites: Dugald Blew   1
Total   1

Whites: Archibald Bradly   1
Total   1

Whites: John Boyd Senr.   2
Female Slaves   1
Total   3

Whites: Stephen Bryan   1
Total   1

Whites: David Bryan   1
Total   1

Whites: Edward Bryan   2
Men Slaves   1
Boys   1
Total   4

Amey Bryant
Whites   0
Female Slaves   2
Total   2

Whites: ~~Ezekiel Bryant~~   ~~1~~

Whites: Michael Barns   1
Total   1

Whites: James Bullard   1
Total   1

Whites: William Baker   1
Total   1

Whites: Henry Bird   1
Total   1

Whites: Charles Benbow   3
Female Slaves   1
Boys   2
Total   6

Whites: ~~Benjamin Benbow~~

Whites: ~~Thomas Benbow~~

Whites: ~~Thomas Brown~~

Whites: Thomas Brown   2
Men Slaves   6
Female Slaves   7
Total   15

Whites: ~~John C[?]olson~~

Whites: Duncan Boie   3
Total   3

Whites: William Baxley   1
Total   1

Whites: Edmund Baxley   2
Total   2

Whites: John Botchard   1
Total   1

Whites: John Berry   1
Total   1

Whites: Britton Barnes   1
Total   1

Whites: Benjamin Britt   1
Total   1

Whites: William Blue   1
Total   1

Whites: Neil Brown   1
Total   1

Whites: William Barlow   2
Total   2

Whites: James Briggs   1
Total   1

Whites: Britton Branch	1
Total	1

Whites: Malcom Boie	1
Total	1

Whites: William Butler	2
Total	2

Whites: Neil Brown	2
Men Slaves	1
Total	3

Whites: Hugh Brown	1
Female Slaves	1
Total	2

Whites: Angus Brown	1
Total	1

Whites: John Baxley	2
Total	2

Whites: Thomas Budd	1
Total	1

Whites: William Brumble	1
Total	1

Whites: Ambrose Bullard	1
Total	1

Whites: Charles Bullock	1
Total	1

Whites: Abram Barnes	1
Men Slaves	1
Female Slaves	1
Total	3

Whites: Samuel Britt	1
Total	1

Whites: Stephen Butler	2
Men Slaves	1
Female Slaves	2
Total	5

Whites: James Beard	1
Men Slaves	2
Total	3

Whites: Samuel Boazman	2
Total	2

Whites: James Bennit	1
Total	1

Whites: Samuel Boazman	2
Total	2

Whites: John Beard	2
Men Slaves	1
Total	3

Whites: Daniel Beard	1
Total	1

Whites: Samuel Butler	1
Men Slaves	3
Female Slaves	1
Total	5

Whites: Joseph Butler	1
Men Slaves	1
Total	2

Whites: Thomas Browder	1
Total	1

Whites: John Baldwin	1
Men Slaves	1
Female Slaves	1
Total	3

Whites: William Brown	1
Total	1

Whites: John Branton	3
Total	3

Whites: John Butler	1
Total	1

Whites: Thomas Bryan	
Men Slaves	1
Female Slaves	1
Total	2

Whites: Luke Barefield	2
Men Slaves	1
Female Slaves	6
Total	9

Whites: William Boyets	2
Total	2

Whites: Simon Bright	2
Total	2

Whites: James Brown	1
Total	1

Whites: Ezekiel Busby	1
Total	1

Whites: William Busby	1
Total	1

Whites: Jeremiah Bigford	2
Female Slaves	2
Total	4

Whites: William Bryan	3
Female Slaves	1
Total	4

Whites: James Benson	1
Total	1

Whites: Peter Broadas	1
Men Slaves	3
Boys	1
Total	5

Whites: Jesse Blackwell	2
Total	2

Whites: Charles Barker	1
Total	1

Whites: Moses Butler	1
Total	1

Whites: David Barefield	2
Total	2

Whites: William Boss	1
Total	1

Whites: William Butler	2
Total	2

Whites: Miles Barefield	3
Total	3

Whites: John Blount	3
Men Slaves	1
Total	4

Whites: Jacob Blount	1
Total	1

Whites: James Blount	1
Total	1

Whites: Philip Blount	1
Total	1

Whites: Joseph Baggett	1
Total	1

Whites: Edmund Brown	1
Total	1

Whites: Charles Barefield	1
Total	1

Whites: William Bird	1
Total	1

Jean Bryan
Whites	0
Female Slaves	1
Total	1

Margaret Byrn
Whites	1
Men Slaves	3
Female Slaves	4
Boys	2
Total	10

Whites: Peter Byrn	4
Total	4

Whites: Robert Baker	1
Men Slaves	1
Total	2

Whites: James Bailey	3
Men Slaves	6
Female Slaves	2
Total	11

Whites: John Baldwin	2
Men Slaves	3
Female Slaves	2
Boys	1
Total	8

Whites: Charles Baldwin	1
Men Slaves	1
Female Slaves	1
Total	3

Whites: James Baldwin	1
Men Slaves	1
Female Slaves	1
Total	3

Whites: Maurice Biben	3
Total	3

Whites: William Burney	1
Men Slaves	2
Female Slaves	2
Total	5

Whites: William Burney	1
Total	1

Whites: Joseph Baldwin	1
Total	1

Whites: William Barefoot	1
Men Slaves	6
Female Slaves	8
Total	15

Whites: Benjamin Beesly	1
Total	1

Whites: Joseph Britton	1
Men Slaves	8
Female Slaves	13
Total	22

Whites: John Best	2
Total	2

Whites: Lazarus Creel	2
Total	2

Whites: James Carter	3
Total	3

Whites: Robert Clyburn	1
Total	1

Whites: William Clapps	1
Total	1

Whites: Joseph Cain	1
Men Slaves	2
Female Slaves	1
Total	4

Whites: Maturin Colvill	1
Men Slaves	11
Female Slaves	12
Boys	2
Total	26

Whites: James Councell	1
Men Slaves	2
Female Slaves	3
Total	6

Whites: John Cain	1
Men Slaves	1
Total	2

Whites: William Cain	1
Men Slaves	5
Female Slaves	4
Total	10

Whites: John Caid	1
Men Slaves	1
Female Slaves	2
Total	4

Whites: Angus Cameron	1
Total	1

Whites: Samuel Cain	1
Men Slaves	1
Total	2

Whites: William Crowson	1
Total	1

Whites: Peter Carpenter	2
Total	2

Whites: Daniel Curry	2
Total	2

Whites: Robert Carlile	1
Total	1

Whites: John Coleman	1
Total	1

Whites: Maurice Coleman	1
Total	1

Whites: David Clark	1
Total	1

Whites: Benjamin Clark	2
Total	2

Whites: William Cain	3
Total	3

Whites: Henry Clark	1
Total	1

Chapter 6: Bladen County Tax Lists of 1774

Whites: Samuel Carman	1
Total	1

Whites: William Cromarty	1
Men Slaves	1
Female Slaves	1
Total	3

Whites: John Chewell	1
Total	1

Whites: Thomas Chewell	1
Total	1

Whites: Benjamin Clark	2
Men Slaves	2
Female Slaves	1
Boys	1
Total	6

Whites: Josiah Carter	2
Total	2

Whites: Jesse Carter	1
Total	1

Whites: Dennis Coleman	1
Total	1

Whites: Neil Colbreath	1
Total	1

Whites: Duncan Campbell	3
Men Slaves	1
Total	4

Whites: Isaac Cannady	1
Total	1

Whites: Thomas Creel	1
Total	1

Whites: Sampson Carver	1
Men Slaves	2
Female Slaves	1
Total	4

Whites: Samuel Canady	1
Men Slaves	1
Female Slaves	2
Total	4

Whites: Samuel Canady Junr.	1
Total	1

Whites: Daniel Campbell	1
Total	1

Whites: Abel Corbet	1
Total	1

Whites: Joseph Cooper	1
Men Slaves	1
Female Slaves	1
Total	3

Whites: Simon Cork[?]	2
Total	2

Whites: Gilbert Cox	2
Total	2

Whites: Absalom Collings	1
Total	1

Whites: Richard Chesher	3
Total	3

Whites: Benony Clayton	1
Men Slaves	1
Total	2

Whites: Daniel Curry	1
Total	1

Whites: Issoms Chiles	2
Total	2

Whites: John Campbell	2
Men Slaves	5
Female Slaves	11
Boys	1

Whites: John Carsey	2
Men Slaves	1
Total	3

Whites: William Cook	1
Total	1

Whites: Samuel Curry	1
Total	1

Whites: John Campbell	2
Total	2

Whites: Thomas Cox	2
Total	2

Chapter 6: Bladen County Tax Lists of 1774

Whites: James Clardy	3
Men Slaves	3
Female Slaves	3
Boys	1
Total	10

Whites: John Cohoon	2
Total	2

Whites: James Cohoon	1
Total	1

Whites: John Chancey	2
Total	2

Whites: John Clark	1
Total	1

Whites: Daniel Cohoon	1
Total	1

Widow Corbet	
Whites	1
Total	1

Whites: John Dois [Dors]	1
Total	1

Whites: James Dupree	1
Men Slaves	6
Female Slaves	5
Total	12

Whites: Morgan Drury	1
Total	1

Whites: Thomas Davis	1
Total	1

Whites: Kelly Dedge	1
Total	1

Whites: John Dorman	1
Total	1

Whites: William Dunn	1
Total	1

Whites: Hester Dean	2
Total	2

Whites: John Dreddin	1
Total	1

The headings in this document for Men Slaves & Female Slaves has changed to B. Males & B. Females.

Whites: William Davis	2
B. Females	1
Total	3

Whites: Edward Davis	1
B. Females	2
Total	3

Whites: William Dowlas	2
Total	2

Whites: Archibald Darrah	2
B. Males	1
Total	3

Whites: Charles Dent	2
Total	2

Whites: John Devesters	1
Total	1

Whites: Dennis Dorson	1
B. Males	1
B. Females	1
Total	3

Whites: Thomas Dyson	1
Total	1

Whites: Solomon Dyson	1
Total	1

Whites: David Duncan	1
B. Males	1
B. Females	1
Total	3

Whites: Elias Duncan	1
Total	1

Whites: Thomas Davis	3
Total	3

Whites: Jeremiah Doan	2
Total	2

Whites: James Dowey	1
Total	1

Whites: Hezekiah Davis	1
B. Males	1
B. Females	1
Boys	2
Total	5

Whites: John Dunbar	1
Total	1

Whites: Samuel Dunn	1
Total	1

Whites: James [Turner] Davis	1
Total	1

Whites: Jeremiah Daffern	1
B. Males	3
B. Females	1
Total	5

Whites: Baxter Davis	2
Total	2

Whites: John Duncan	1
Total	1

Whites: John Everett	1
Total	1

Whites: James Evers	1
Total	1

Whites: Evin Ellis	1
B. Males	1
B. Females	1
Total	3

Whites: Lewis Everett	1
Total	1

Whites: William Ellis	1
B. Males	1
Total	2

Whites: William Edwards	1
Total	1

Whites: Samuel Edwards	1
Total	1

Whites: Samuel Evens [Evers]	1
Total	1

Whites: Absalom Etheridge	1
Total	1

Whites: Richard Elwell	2
Total	2

Whites: James Ellis	1
B. Males	5
B. Females	1
Total	7

Whites: John Ellis	1
Total	1

Whites: John Ellis Senr.	2
B. Males	2
B. Females	2
Boys	1
Total	7

Whites: Robert Edwards	2
B. Males	2
B. Females	2
Total	6

Whites: Joseph Edwards	1
Total	1

Whites: James Fokes	1
Total	1

Whites: Elias Fort	1
B. Males	1
B. Females	1
Total	3

Whites: Dempsey Fiveash	2
Total	2

Benjamin Fitzrandolph	
Whites	0
B. Males	1
B. Females	1
Total	2

Whites: William Forrester	1
Total	1

Whites: John Fokes	2
Total	2

Whites: Daniel Flin	1
Total	1

Whites: Joseph Fort	1
B. Males	2
B. Females	4
Total	7

Whites: Benjamin Freeman	1
Total	1

Whites: Edward Flowers	5
Total	5

Whites: William Farrell	1
Total	1

Whites: William Freeman	1
Total	1

Whites: George Fletcher	2
B. Males	1
B. Females	2
Total	5

Whites: Stephen Freeman	1
Total	1

Whites: Thomas Freeman	1
Total	1

Whites: James Farquerson	2
Total	2

Whites: John Fowler	1
Total	1

Whites: Josiah Flandon	1
B. Males	3
B. Females	1
Total	5

Whites: John Faris	1
Total	1

Whites: John Faisly	3
Total	3

Whites: Isaac Grooms	1
Total	1

Whites: Andrew Griffin	3
B. Males	1
Total	4

Whites: Richard Grantham	1
Total	1

Whites: Jacob Gyton	2
B. Males	2
Total	4

Whites: William Groom	1
Total	1

Whites: Edward Grantham	1
B. Males	1
Total	2

Whites: James Grantham	1
Total	1

Whites: Jonas Gadin	1
Total	1

Whites: John Green	1
B. Males	1
Total	2

Whites: William Garrard	1
B. Males	3
B. Females	1
Total	5

Whites: Walter Gibson	2
B. Males	3
B. Females	6
Boys	1
Total	12

Whites: Alexander Graham	2
Total	2

Whites: Caleb Galloway	2
Total	2

Faithful Graham	
Whites	2
B. Males	2
B. Females	2
Total	6

Whites: James Giffard	1
Total	1

Whites: Abraham Gray	1
Total	1

Whites: Christopher Goodwin	1
Total	1

Isaac Grooms	
[No Listings Given.]	

Whites: Samuel Guyton	1
Total	1

Whites: William Godfrey	1
Total	1

Whites: John Gilcrease	1
Total	1

Whites: Alexander Grimes	2
Total	2

Whites: John Green	1
B. Males	1
Total	2

Whites: William Green	2
B. Males	2
B. Females	1
Total	5

Margaret Gibbs	
Whites	0
B. Males	4
B. Females	5
Total	9

Whites: James Green	1
Total	1

Whites: Andrew Graham	1
Total	1

Whites: Robert Grice	1
Total	1

Whites: Levy Glass	2
B. Males	1
B. Females	2
Total	5

Whites: Thomas Groom	1
Total	1

Whites: Burrell Haregrove	1
Total	1

Whites: William Hubbard	1
Total	1

Whites: Edward Haley	2
Total	2

Whites: Josiah Handon	1
B. Males	3
B. Females	1
Total	5

Whites: John Harrison Junr.	4
B. Males	2
B. Females	3
Total	9

Whites: Thomas Howard	1
Total	1

Whites: Stephen Hesters	1
Total	1

Whites: John Hill	1
Total	1

Whites: William Handon	2
B. Females	1
Boys	2
Total	5

[The headings in this list have changed from B. Males and B. Females to B. Men and B. Women.]

Whites: Thomas Hesters	3
Total	3

Whites: William Hesters	1
Total	1

Whites: Benjamin Humphreys	2
B. Women	1
Total	3

Whites: Alexander Harvey	3
Total	3

Whites: Thomas Hardick	1
Total	1

Whites: Jacob Hanchy	1
Total	1

Whites: Ezekiel Hill	2
Total	2

Whites: Thomas Hays	1
Total	1

Whites: Thomas Harwick	2
Total	2

Whites: Ducan Henderson	1
Total	1

Whites: Joshua Hays	2
Total	2

Whites: Hudnell Huffum	1
Total	1

Whites: Richard Huffum	1
Total	1

Whites: John Howard	2
B. Men	2
B. Women	2
Total	6

Whites: Benjamin Howard	1
B. Men	1
Total	1

Whites: William Hargrove	1
Total	1

Whites: Ezekiel Howard	1
Total	1

Whites: Moses Holmes	1
Total	1

Whites: William Horn[?]	1
B. Men	1
Total	2

Whites: John Harrison	1
B. Men	1
Total	2

Whites: Richard Harrison	1
B. Males	1
Total	2

Whites: Abel Houlton	2
B. Men	1
Total	3

Whites: Thomas Holford	1
Total	1

Whites: Samuel Hails	1
Total	1

Whites: Richard Hammonds	2
B. Men	3
B. Women	1
Total	6

Whites: Stephen Hollingsworth	1
Total	1

Whites: John Hollingsworth	1
Total	1

Whites: Nathan Horne	1
Total	1

Whites: George Harrell	1
Total	1

Whites: Jesse Harrell	2
B. Men	1
B. Women	1
Total	4

Whites: Elisha Harrell	1
B. Men	1
B. Women	2
Total	4

Whites: Chambers Humphrey	1
Total	1

Whites: Ralph Howell	1
Total	1

Whites: William Horne	3
Total	3

Whites: Belitha Hays	3
B. Men	1
Total	4

Whites: Enoch Hall	1
Total	1

Whites: Isaac Hall	1
Total	1

Whites: Joseph Hopkins	1
Total	1

Whites: Thomas Jackson	1
Total	1

Whites: Lewis Jenkins	1
Total	1

Whites: John Jackson	1
Total	1

Whites: William Jones	1
Total	1

Whites: William Johnston	3
Total	3

Whites: James Isham	1
B. Men	1
Total	2

Whites: John Jones	2
B. Women	3
Boys	1
Total	6

Whites: Isaac Jones	3
B. Men	3
B. Women	2
Total	8

Whites: William Johnson	2
Total	2

Whites: Nehemiah Johnson	2
Total	2

Whites: Thomas Johnson	1
Total	1

Whites: John Johnson Senr.	1
Total	1

Whites: Philip Ikener	3
Total	3

Whites: John Johnson	1
Total	1

Whites: Thomas Jackson	1
Total	1

Dorothy Ikener	
Whites	0
B. Men	1
Total	1

Whites: James Jackson	1
B. Men	1
Total	2

Whites: Thomas Ivey	1
Total	1

Whites: Isham Ivey	1
Total	1

Whites: Hardy Inman	3
Total	3

Whites: James Inman	2
Total	2

Whites: Solomon James	2
Total	2

Whites: Jeremiah Ivey	1
Total	1

Whites: Thomas Jennings	1
Total	1

Whites: John Jarvis	1
Total	1

Whites: Isaac Jessup	1
Total	1

~~**Whites**: Benjamin Ivey~~	~~1~~

Whites: John Kennady	1
Total	1

Margrett Kees [**Keer**]	
Whites	0
B. Men	1
Total	1

Whites: Matthew Kelly	1
B. Men	3
B. Women	2
Total	6

Whites: Archibald Kelly	1
Total	1

Whites: John Kannon	1
Total	1

Whites: Joseph Kemp	1
B. Women	1
Total	2

Whites: Thomas Kinlaw	1
Total	1

Whites: John King	1
B. Men	1
Boys	1
Total	3

Whites: Wm Kirkpatrick	1
B. Men	1
B. Women	1
Total	3

Whites: Abraham King	1
Total	1

Whites: John Lennon	2
Total	2

Whites: John Leggett	7
B. Men	3
B. Women	1
Total	11

Whites: Archibald Little	1
Total	1

Whites: Duncan Little	1
Total	1

Whites: Absalom Leggett	2
Total	2

Whites: John Little	1
Total	1

Whites: Uriah Lamberthson	1
Total	1

Whites: John Lock	2
B. Men	2
B. Women	3
Total	7

Whites: William Lee	1
Total	1

Whites: Gutteredge Lockaleer	1
Total	1

Whites: Isaac Lamb	3
Total	3

Whites: Arther Lamb	1
Total	1

Whites: Thoms Little	3
Total	3

Whites: Shaderic Lee	2
Total	2

Whites: Dennis Lennon	1
B. Men	1
Total	2

Whites: James Lewis Senr.	3
Total	3

Whites: Josiah Lewis Senr.	2
B. Females	2
Total	4

Whites: Francis Lawson	2
Total	2

Whites: George Long	1
Total	1

Whites: Richard Lloyd	1
B. Men	1
B. Women	1
Total	3

Whites: David Lock	3
B. Men	2
B. Women	2
Total	7

Whites: Francis Lucas	1
B. Men	2
B. Women	3
Boys	1
Total	7

Whites: David Lloyd	2
Total	2

Whites: Joseph Lock	2
B. Men	1
B. Women	1
Total	4

Whites: Peter Lord	4
B. Men	3
B. Women	2
Total	9

Whites: John Lucas	2
B. Men	6
B. Women	6
Boys	1
Total	15

Whites: William Hall	1
Total	1

Whites: Hanson Lewis	2
B. Men	1
B. Women	1
Total	4

Whites: Benjamin Lambethson	2
B. Men	2
B. Women	3
Total	7

Whites: Thomas Lock	1
B. Men	2
Total	3

Whites: Solomon Lewis	1
Total	1

Whites: Zachariah Lee	1
B. Women	1
Total	2

Whites: Lewis Hall	3
Total	3

Whites: John McCononlay	1
Total	1

Whites: Samuel McRee	1
B. Men	2
Total	3

Whites: Thomas Mims	2
B. Men	2
Total	4

Whites: Ralph Miller	2
B. Men	2
B. Women	4
Boys	1
Total	9

Whites: John Moore	1
B. Men	1
B. Women	1
Total	3

Whites: Jacob Mesick	2
Total	2

Whites: Thomas McGuire	2
B. Men	16
B. Women	18
Boys	3
Total	39

Whites: Basil Manley	1
B. Men	15
B. Women	11
Boys	1
Total	28

Whites: Berringer Moore	2
B. Men	13
B. Women	13
Total	28

Whites: Daniel McKinsey	1
Total	1

Whites: Mathew Muns	1
Total	1

Whites: William Moorehead	2
B. Men	1
B. Women	1
Total	4

Whites: John Moore	1
Total	1

Whites: John McNeil	1
Total	1

Whites: Solomon Messer Senr.	1
B. Men	1
Total	2

Whites: Solomon Messer Junr.	1
Total	1

Whites: John McLeod	1
Total	1

Whites: Nathan Meredith	1
Total	1

Whites: Daniel McKock[?]	2
B. Men	1
Total	3

Whites: Michael Mix[?]n	1
Total	1

Mary McDugal	
Whites	1
Total	1

Whites: Ephraim Mulford	1
B. Men	1
B. Women	1
Total	3

Whites: Peter Meshaw	1
Total	1

Whites: Daniel Melvin	1
Total	1

Whites: Archibald McLain	1
Total	1

Whites: Thomas Mustlewhite	2
B. Men	1
Total	3

Whites: Malakiah Messer	1
Total	1

Whites: Daniel Maclain	1
B. Men	1
B. Women	1
Total	3

Whites: Joseph Messer	1
B. Men	1
Total	2

Whites: Joshua Messer	1
Total	1

Whites: John McDonald	1
Total	1

Whites: William Moore	1
Total	1

Whites: Jacob Munts	1
Total	1

Whites: Archibald McBride	2
B. Men	1
Total	3

Whites: James Murphey	1
Total	1

Whites: Alexander McGillop	1
Total	1

Whites: Robert McConkey	2
B. Men	1
B. Women	1
Total	4

Whites: William Maulsby	2
Total	2

Ann Maulsby

Whites	1
B. Men	2
B. Women	2
Total	5

Whites: Thomas McClelland	1
Total	1

Whites: Archibald McColesky	3
B. Women	2
Total	5

Whites: Duncan McKeithan	1
B. Men	1
B. Women	1
Total	3

Mary McFatter

Whites	2
Total	2

Whites: Archibald McKeithan	1
Total	1

Mary McClelland

Whites	3
B. Men	1
B. Women	1
Boys	1
Total	6

Whites: Gilbert McKeithan	1
Total	1

Whites: Donold McKeithan	1
Total	1

Whites: Daniel McFatter	1
Total	1

Whites: Angus McCoy	1
B. Men	1
Total	2

Whites: John McKinsey	3
Total	3

Whites: Neil McColesky	2
B. Women	1
Total	3

Whites: Iver McCoy	1
B. Men	4
B. Women	4
Total	9

Whites: Alexander McLarty	3
Total	3

Whites: William McRee	1
B. Men	6
B. Women	3
Total	10

Whites: Charles McNaugten	1
Total	1

Whites: John McDaniel	1
Total	1

Whites: William McMaster	1
Total	1

Whites: Robert McRee	2
B. Men	1
Total	3

Whites: James Moore	1
B. Men	1
B. Women	1
Total	3

Whites: Daniel McNicols	2
Total	2

Whites: James Money	3
Total	3

Amelia Marley	
Whites	0
B. Men	2
B. Women	1
Total	3

Elizabeth McKay	
Whites	1
Total	1

Whites: Daniel McCullom	1
Total	1

Whites: John McKnown	3
Total	3

Whites: William McNeil	2
B. Men	2
B. Women	2
Total	6

Whites: Daniel Mathis	1
Total	1

Whites: Ever McMillin	2
Total	2

Whites: William McFatter	1
Total	1

Whites: Hector McNeil	1
B. Men	2
B. Women	1
Total	4

Whites: James Mash	1
Total	1

Whites: Godfrey McNeil	1
Total	1

Whites: William Moore	1
Total	1

Whites: Peter McArther	1
Total	1

Whites: Peter McKeller	1
Total	1

Whites: John Moore	1
Total	1

Whites: Malcom Munroe	1
Total	1

Whites: Neil McNickols	1
Total	1

Whites: Murdoch McLoud	1
Total	1

Whites: Jesse Moss	1
Total	1

Whites: Turtle McNeil	2
B. Men	4
B. Women	2
Total	8

Whites: Neil McFall		2
B. Men		1
B. Women		1
Total		4

Whites: Daniel Mclaughlen		1
Total		1

Whites: John McCrayney		2
B. Men		1
Total		3

Whites: Daniel McDuffie		1
Total		1

Whites: Lewis Munroe		1
B. Men		1
Total		2

Whites: Daniel McAtager		1
Total		1

Whites: Henry Mercer		2
B. Men		1
B. Women		1
Total		4

Whites: John McFarson		4
B. Men		2
B. Women		2
Total		8

Whites: Jesse Mustlewhite		1
Total		1

Whites: Christopher McKay		2
Total		2

Whites: William Miller		1
Total		1

Whites: Daniel McSwain		1
Total		1

Whites: James McNeil		1
B. Men		2
B. Women		1
Total		4

Whites: Neil McNeil		1
B. Men		1
B. Women		1
Total		3

Whites: Alexander McLoud		1
Total		1

Whites: Malcom McNeil		1
Total		1

Whites: Hector McNeil, Sailor		1
Total		1

Whites: Daniel McEacharn		1
Total		1

Whites: Milby Mustlewhite		1
Total		1

Whites: Hugh McCrayney		3
B. Men		1
B. Women		1
Total		5

Whites: Gilbert McCormach		1
Total		1

Whites: John McCormach		1
Total		1

Whites: Archibald McCormach		1
Total		1

Whites: James McDaniel		2
B. Men		2
B. Women		1
Total		5

Whites: Noah Mercer		1
Total		1

Whites: John Mercer Senr		2
Total		2

Whites: Daniel McLain		2
Total		2

Whites: James Moore		1
Total		1

Whites: Archibald McKissak		2
B. Men		2
B. Women		1
Total		5

Whites: Joseph Melton		1
Total		1

Whites: Malcom McFatter		1
Total		1

Whites: Roger Neil	1
Total	1

Whites: Coleman Nickes	1
B. Men	2
B. Women	1
Total	4

Whites: Joseph Noble	1
Total	1

Whites: John Newberry	2
B. Men	2
B. Women	1
Total	5

Whites: Jesse Newberry	1
B. Men	5
B. Women	4
Total	10

Whites: John Newberry Senr.	1
B. Women	1
Total	2

Whites: John Nicklason	3
Total	3

Whites: William Oliphant Const.	0
B. Men	5
B. Women	1
Total	6

Whites: Jesse Oliphant	1
Total	1

Whites: Aaron Odom	2
Total	2

Whites: Tarlow Oguin	2
Total	2

Whites: Tarlow Oguin Junr.	1
Total	1

Whites: Hardy Oguin	1
Total	1

Whites: Joseph Oats	1
B. Men	2
B. Women	1
Total	4

Whites: Carraway Oats Constable	0
Total	0

Whites: William Owen	1
B. Men	1
B. Women	2
Total	4

Whites: Thomas Owen	2
B. Men	11
B. Women	5
Total	18

Whites: John Owen	3
B. Men	7
B. Women	4
Total	14

Whites: John Odom	3
Total	3

Whites: John Pointer	2
B. Men	2
Total	4

Whites: John Powell Senr	2
B. Men	2
B. Women	1
Boys	1
Total	6

Whites: Sampson Pope	1
B. Men	1
B. Women	1
Total	3

Whites: Henry Pope	1
B. Women	1
Total	2

Whites: John Phillips	1
Total	1

Whites: Mathew Pridgen	4
Total	4

Whites: Jeremiah Plumer	1
Total	1

Whites: John Parker	1
B. Women	1
Total	2

Whites: Gidion Pricket	1
Total	1

Whites: John Plumer	3
Total	3

Whites: Joseph Powers	2
Total	2

Whites: Andrew Puffs	1
Total	1

Whites: Benjamin Powell	1
Total	1

Whites: Ambrose Powell	1
Total	1

Whites: Charles Powell	1
Total	1

Whites: Joseph Powell	2
Total	2

Whites: Daniel Paterson	1
Total	1

Whites: Josiah Powell	2
Total	2

Whites: James Pate	1
Total	1

Whites: Abram Paul	1
Total	1

Whites: Joel Pittman	1
Total	1

Whites: Jesse Pittman	2
Total	2

Whites: Thomas Pittman	2
B. Men	1
B. Women	1
Total	4

Whites: Sampson Pittman	1
Total	1

Whites: William Purcell	4
Total	4

Whites: John Pemberton Constable	1
B. Women	1
Total	2

Whites: Samuel Rourk	1
B. Men	1
Total	2

Whites: Thomas Richards	1
Total	1

Whites: John Rowland	1
Men Slaves	1
Women Slaves	1
Total	3

Whites: James Rowland	5
Total	5

Whites: John Regan	2
Total	2

Whites: Joseph Regan	1
Men Slaves	3
Women Slaves	2
Total	6

Whites: Thomas Russ	1
Men Slaves	1
Women Slaves	1
Boys	1
Total	4

Whites: John Russ	3
Men Slaves	1
Total	4

Whites: Thomas Robeson Senr.	2
Men Slaves	3
Women Slaves	5
Boys	2
Total	12

Whites: Thomas Robeson Junr.	2
Men Slaves	8
Women Slaves	3
Total	13

Whites: John Roberts	2
Total	2

Whites: Peter Robeson	1
Women Slaves	1
Total	2

Whites: ~~Reuben Roberts~~	

Whites: James Richards	3
Men Slaves	5
Women Slaves	4
Total	12

Whites: Robert Richardson	2
Total	2

Chapter 6:   Bladen County Tax Lists of 1774

Whites: John Rogerson	2
Men Slaves	2
Women Slaves	1
Total	5
Whites: Samuel Rowan	1
Total	1
Whites: Joseph Ray	1
Total	1
Whites: David Richards	2
Total	2
Whites: Edward Reeves Constable	0
Total	0
Whites: Nathaniel Reve	1
Women Slaves	1
Boys	1
Total	3
Whites: Isaac Ray	2
Men Slaves	2
Women Slaves	3
Total	7
Whites: John Richardson	2
Total	2
Whites: John Roger	2
Total	2
Whites: Charles Rabourn	1
Total	1
Whites: Thomas Rowland	1
Total	1
Whites: John Raiborn	1
Total	1
Whites: John Rosher	1
Total	1
Whites: Reuben Rosher	3
Total	3
Whites: David Rosher	1
Total	1
Whites: Gilbert Ramsey	2
Total	2

Whites: Isaac Rosher	4
Total	4
Whites: Thomas Russel	1
Total	1
Whites: Ralph Regan	1
Total	1
Whites: James Riseng	1
Total	1
Whites: Nathaniel Richardson	2
Men Slaves	5
Women Slaves	4
Total	11
Whites: William Russ	1
Total	1
Whites: David Russ, patrole	0
Total	0
Whites: John Russ	2
Total	2
Whites: William Runnels	2
Men Slaves	1
Women Slaves	1
Total	4
Whites: William Smith	4
Men Slaves	2
Total	6
Whites: Daniel Shaw	3
Men Slaves	1
Women Slaves	1
Total	4
Whites: John Shaw	2
Total	2
Sarah Seymore	
Whites	1
Total	1
Whites: William Singletary	3
Men Slaves	1
Women Slaves	1
Total	5

Chapter 6:   Bladen County Tax Lists of 1774

Mary Singletary	
Whites	1
Men Slaves	1
Women Slaves	1
Total	3

Whites: Neil Shaw	2
Men Slaves	2
Women Slaves	1
Total	5

Whites: Archibald Shaw	1
Total	1

Whites: John Smith	2
Men Slaves	6
Women Slaves	5
Total	13

Whites: Richard Small	1
Total	1

Whites: Richard Singletary	3
Men Slaves	4
Women Slaves	1
Boys	1
Total	9

Whites: Peter Simon	2
Total	2

Whites: James Stewart	1
Total	1

Whites: John Sewester	1
Total	1

Whites: Robert Sims	1
Total	1

Whites: John Smith	1
Total	1

Whites: James Smith	1
Total	1

Whites: John Smith Junr.	1
Total	1

Whites: Tobias Seald	1
Total	1

Whites: William Smith	1
Total	1

Whites: Thomas Starling	2
Total	2

Whites: John Smith	1
Men Slaves	11
Women Slaves	11
Boys	2
Total	25

Whites: Samuel Smith	1
Men Slaves	1
Women Slaves	2
Total	4

Whites: Benjamin Sims	1
Total	1

Whites: Barnibas Stevens	2
Men Slaves	3
Women Slaves	1
Total	6

Whites: Joshua Stevens	2
Men Slaves	2
Women Slaves	1
Total	5

Whites: William Strickling	2
Total	2

Whites: Christopher Sanders	2
Total	2

Whites: Willis Stedephant	1
Total	1

Whites: Matthew Sellers	1
Total	1

Whites: Thomas Sanders Senr.	3
Men Slaves	1
Women Slaves	1
Total	5

Whites: Thomas Simson	1
Women Slaves	3
Total	4

Whites: John Simson	1
Total	1

Whites: James Shipman	2
Men Slaves	1
Total	3

Chapter 6: Bladen County Tax Lists of 1774

Whites: Angus Sellers	3
Total	3
Whites: Richard Singletary	2
Men Slaves	1
Women Slaves	1
Total	4
Whites: Christopher Sutton	2
Total	2
Whites: Thomas Suggs	1
Total	1
Whites: Thomas Sussoms	1
Total	1
Whites: John Sellers	3
Total	3
Whites: John Smith	2
Total	2
Whites: John Suggs	1
Total	1
Whites: James Singletary	1
Total	1
Whites: John Storm	1
Total	1
Whites: John Sizmore	1
Total	1
Whites: Samuel Sutton	3
Total	3
Whites: Richard Salter	4
Men Slaves	2
Women Slaves	1
Total	7
Whites: Isaac Sims	3
Men Slaves	2
Total	5
Whites: Thomas Scriven	1
Total	1
Elizabeth Singletary	
Whites:	1
Men Slaves	1
Total	2

Whites: Othniel Straughan	2
Men Slaves	1
Total	3
Whites: William Stewart	3
Men Slaves	7
Women Slaves	6
Boys	4
Total	20
Whites: John Sykes	1
Total	1
Whites: Jacob Sykes	2
Total	2
Whites: Josiah Sykes	1
Total	1
Whites: Robert Stewart	2
Men Slaves	1
Women Slaves	3
Total	6
Whites: William Salter	3
Men Slaves	8
Women Slaves	4
Boys	2
Total	17
Whites: Beaumont Sutton	2
Men Slaves	1
Total	3
Whites: John Sutton	1
Total	1
Whites: William Shaw	2
Total	2
Whites: Richard Smith	1
Women Slaves	2
Total	3
Whites: John Starling	2
Women Slaves	1
Total	3
Whites: Thomas Smith	2
Women Slaves	1
Total	3
Grace Smith	
Whites	1
Men Slaves	1
Total	2

Whites: William Starkey	1
Total	1

Whites: John Stubbs Senr	2
Total	2

Whites: Richard Stubbs	1
Total	1

Whites: John Smith	4
Total	4

Whites: Arthur Smith	1
Total	1

[Name blotted out]

Whites: Archibald Smith	1
Total	1

Whites: Abraham Strickland	1
Total	1

Whites: John Tailor	1
Total	1

Whites: Harburt Tailor	1
Total	1

Whites: Jonathan Taylor	2
Total	2

Whites: Benjamin Thomas	1
Total	1

Whites: George Thomas	3
Total	3

Whites: Moses Treadway	2
Women Slaves	1
Total	3

Whites: John Turner	2
Men Slaves	6
Women Slaves	5
Total	13

Whites: Michael Thomas	1
Total	1

Whites: Aaron Tomlinson	2
Total	2

Whites: Israel Tomlinson	1
Total	1

Whites: William Taylor	1
Total	1

Whites: Joseph Thims	4
Men Slaves	2
Women Slaves	1
Total	7

Whites: Neil Thomas	1
Total	1

Whites: Henry Taylor	2
Total	2

Whites: William Thompson	1
Total	1

Whites: Charles Thomas	2
Total	2

Whites: William Toler	1
Total	1

Whites: Archibald Taylor	4
Total	4

Whites: John Taylor	1
Total	1

Whites: Lewis Thomas	1
Total	1

Whites: Thomas Townsend	2
Total	2

Whites: Thomas Turner	2
Total	2

Mrs. Waddle	
Whites	1
Men Slaves	34
Women Slaves	36
Total	61
[The above total is probably an error.]	

Whites: John White (M)	3
Total	3

Whites: Stephen White	1
Total	1

Whites: David White Senr.	2
Men Slaves	2
Total	4

Margaret Weir	
Whites	1
Total	1

Whites: Isaac Wilks	1
Total	1

Whites: John Ward	1
Total	1

Whites: William Wilkinson	1
Total	1

Whites: James Wilkinson	1
Total	1

Whites: William Wilkinson Senr.	1
Total	1

Whites: Benjamin Willis	4
Women Slaves	2
Total	6

Whites: George Willis	1
Total	1

Whites: Daniel Willis	3
Men Slaves	1
Total	4

Whites: Agerton Willis	4
Men Slaves	16
Women Slaves	11
Total	31

Whites: Edward Wall	1
Total	1

Whites: Edward Wilson	1
Total	1

Whites: James Wilson	1
Total	1

Whites: Alexander Woosides	1
Men Slaves	1
Women Slaves	1
Total	3

Whites: John Wilson	1
Total	1

Whites: Robert Walker	2
Total	2

Whites: William White	1
Men Slaves	4
Total	5

Mary White	
Whites	1
Women Slaves	2
Total	3

Whites: Richard Wilkinson	1
Men Slaves	1
Total	1

Whites: James West Senr.	2
Men Slaves	1
Total	3

Whites: James West Junr.	1
Total	1

Whites: Solomon Wilson	2
Men Slaves	4
Women Slaves	1
Boys	1
Total	8

Whites: David Linsey White	1
Men Slaves	2
Women Slaves	2
Total	5

Whites: Cade Wethersby	2
Women Slaves	1
Total	3

Whites: Griffith Jones White Constable	0
Total	0

Whites: Robert Wells	2
Men Slaves	2
Women Slaves	1
Boys	1
Total	6

Whites: James Washburn	3
Total	3

Whites: Joseph Wood Patrole	0
Men Slaves	1
Total	1

Whites: Philip Wood Constable	0
Men Slaves	1
Total	1

Sarah Wilson

Whites	1
Men Slaves	1
Women Slaves	2
Boys	1
Total	5

Whites: James White	1
Men Slaves	6
Women Slaves	4
Total	11

Whites: John Wilson	2
Total	2

Whites: Joseph Williams	1
Total	1

Whites: Edmund Winfield	1
Total	1

Whites: Joseph White	1
Women Slaves	2
Total	3

Whites: John White	1
Total	1

Whites: William White	2
Men Slaves	1
Women Slaves	1
Total	4

Whites: William Wilkerson	1
Total	1

Whites: Solomon Whitley	1
Total	1

Whites: John Watson	1
Total	1

Whites: Robert Upton	1
Total	1

Whites: David Upton	1
Total	1

Whites: David Young	2
Total	2

Whites: George Young Junr.	1
Total	1

Whites: George Young	1
Total	1

Whites: John Yates	1
Total	1

Whites: Levy Young	3
Men Slaves	1
Women Slaves	1
Total	5

Whites: Peter Yates	3
Total	3

The Title for the last column of names is "Mixt Blood."

The Headings have changed to Males, Females, Male Slaves, Female Slaves, Boys and Total.

James B. Lowery

Males	1
Females	1
Male Slaves	1
Total	3

Jesse Brook

Males	2
Total	2

David Braveboy

Males	1
Females	2
Total	3

William Mitchel

Males	1
Total	1

Titus Overton

Males	1
Females	1
Total	2

John Johnson

Males	1
Females	1
Total	2

Cannon Cumbo

Males	1
Total	1

Ishmael Chivers
Males 1
Total 1

John Hammons
Males 1
Females 1
Total 2

Adam Ivey
Males 2
Total 2

Thomas Ivey
Males 1
Total 1

Thomas Kersey
Males 2
Male Slaves 1
Total 3

Jacob Lockeleir
Males 2
Total 2

William Lockeleir
Males 1
Total 1

John Lockeleir
Males 2
Total 2

Benjamin Ivey
Males 1
Total 1

Elisha Sweetin
Males 2
Female Slaves 2
Total 4

Moses Walker & Wife by William Singletary
Males 1
Females 1
Total 2

John Cumbo
Males 1
Total 1

Isaac Hays
Males 2
Female Slaves 2
Boys 1
Total 5

Samuel Freeman
Males 1
Females 1
Total 2

Joshua Pavey
Males 4
Females 1
Total 5

John Webb
Males 1
Females 2
Total 3

William Freeman
Males 1
Females 1
Total 2

Abraham Freeman
Males 3
Females 1
Total 4

John Blanks
Males 1
Total 1

Charles Pavey
Males 1
Females 1
Total 2

****

BLADEN COUNTY TAX LIST OF 1774

A list of Taxables Taken by John Smith

Headings for this list include: Whites, Black Males, Boys, Females & Total.

Whites: Hudnel Huffam 1
Total 1

Whites: Richard Huffam 1
Total 1

Whites: John McLeod	1
Total	1

Whites: George Thomas & 2 Sons	3
Total	3

Whites: Thomas Davis & 2 Sons William & Thomas	3
Total	3

Whites: John Kannon	1
Total	1

Whites: William Crowson	1
Total	1

Whites: Peter Carpenter & Thos. Ellis	2
Total	2

Elizabeth Singletary
Whites: Son John Singletary and Braton Singletary Constable	1
Black Males	1
Total	2

Whites: Nathan Maradith	1
Total	1

Free Negroes
Isaac Hais	2
Boys	1
Females	2
Total	5

Free Negroes
Samuel Freeman	1
Females	1
Total	2

Whites: John Howard and Son William	2
Black Males	2
Females	2
Total	6

Whites: Othniel Straughan and son Alexander	2
Black Males	1
Total	1

Whites: Benjamin Howard	1
Black Males	1
Total	2

Whites: Daniel McKook and Anguish McKook	2
Black Males	1
Total	3

Whites: William Stewart, Daniel Stewart & Joseph Henery	3
Black Males	7
Boys	4
Females	6
Total	20

Whites: Daniel Curry and John Curry	2
Total	2

Whites: William Hargrove	1
Total	1

Whites: Richard Lloyd	1
Black Males	1
Females	1
Total	3

Whites: Roger Neill	1
Total	1

Whites: James Benson	1
Total	1

Whites: John Sykes	1
Total	1

Whites: Michael Mixson	1
Total	1

Whites: Jacob Sykes & James Gay	2
Total	2

Whites: Josiah Sykes	1
Total	1

Whites: Stephen Anderes	1
Black Males	3
Females	1
Total	5

Whites: David Lock and two Sons	3
Black Males	2
Females	2
Total	7

Whites: Francis Lucas	1
Black Males	2
Boys	1
Females	3
Total	7

Chapter 6: Bladen County Tax Lists of 1774

Whites: ~~Archibald McNeill~~

Whites: David Lloyd & George Thomas Junr. — 2
Total — 2

Whites: Robert Stewart & Archibald McNeal — 2
Black Males — 1
Females — 3
Total — 6

Whites: Jeremiah & Ephraim Doane — 2
Total — 2

Whites: Matthew Pridgen and 3 Sons — 4
Total — 4

Whites: Hezekiah Howard — 1
Total — 1

Whites: Moses Treadway & John Bourdeaux — 2
Females — 1
Total — 3

Whites: John Anderes and Son Constable James Anderes & Benj. Parnel — 3
Black Males — 5
Females — 1
Total — 9

Whites: Peter Broades — 1
Black Males — 3
Females — 1
Total — 5

Whites: Walter Gibson & Alexander Morrison — 2
Black Males — 3
Boys — 1
Females — 6
Total — 12

Whites: Allixander Graham & Murdock Graham — 2
Total — 2

Whites: Thos. Russ — 1
Black Males — 1
Boys — 1
Females — 1
Total — 4

Whites: William Saltar & John & James Saltar — 3
Black Males — 8
Boys — 2
Females — 4
Total — 17

Sarah Wilson & William Streete
Whites — 1
Black Males — 1
Boys — 1
Females — 2
Total — 5

Whites: Joseph Anderes & William Sloan — 2
Total — 2

Mary McDugal & Daniel Mcleod
Whites — 1
Total — 1

Whites: John Russ, Jonadab Russ & Charles Burks — 3
Black Males — 1
Total — 4

Whites: Joseph Lock & Leonard Lock — 2
Black Males — 1
Females — 1
Total — 4

Whites: Ephraim Mulford — 1
Black Males — 1
Females — 3
Total — 5

Whites: Peter Meshaw — 1
Total — 1

Whites: Beaumount Sutton Senior & Junier — 2
Black Males — 1
Total — 3

Whites: John Sutton — 1
Total — 1

Whites: James Dowey — 1
Total — 1

Whites: Hezekiah Davis — 1
Black Males — 1
Boys — 1
Females — 2
Total — 5

Whites: Robert Carlile	1
Total	1

Whites: Jesse Blackwell & William Blackwell	2
Total	2

Whites: Daniel Melvin	1
Total	1

Whites: James White	1
Black Males	6
Females	4
Total	11

Whites: William Shaw & James Shaw	2
Total	2

****

BLADEN COUNTY TAX LIST OF 1774

List of Taxables taken by Thomas Owen in the County of Bladen 1774

Headings in this list include: White Men, Male Slaves, Female Slaves & Boys.

White Men: Philip Ikener & two Sons	3

White Men: Andrew Puff himself	1

White Men: David Young & Son	2

White Men: George Young Junr.	1

White Men: Duncan Boie & Two sons	3

White Men: John Legett & Six Whites	7
Male Slaves	3
Female Slaves	1

White Men: Hecter McNeal	1
Male Slaves	2
Female Slaves	1

White Men: Morgan Drury	1

White Men: William Hubbard	1

White Men: James Mash Himself	1

White Men: John Johnston Himself	1

White Men: Peter Simon & Torquill McLoud	2

White Men: Benjamin Powel Himself	1

White Men: Ambrose Powel	1

White Men: Samuel Evers Himself	1

White Men: Charles Powel Himself	1

White Men: Neal Culbreath Himself	1

White Men: James Stewart Himself	1

White Men: William Godfrey Himself	1

White Men: Godfrey McNeal Himself	1

White Men: Joseph Price Himself & Son	1

White Men: Elias Fort Himself	1
Male Slaves	1
Female Slaves	1

White Men: James Ard Himself	1
Negro Boy	1

White Men: Thomas Davis Himself	1

White Men: William Moore Himself	1

White Men: Peter McArthur Himself	1

White Men: William Baxley Himself	1

White Men: Ruben Ard Himself	1
Female Slave	1

White Men: Peter McKeller Himself	1

White Men: John Moore & Matthew Moore	2

White Men: Edmund Baxley & Joseph Baxley	2

Male Slaves: John Cumbee	1
Female Slaves: John Cumbees Wife Lucy	1

[Even though the two people above are listed as slaves, they are listed elsewhere as free mulattoes.]

White Men: Telly Dedge Himself	1

White Men: John Sewester Himself	1

White Men: John Botchard Himself	1

White Men: William Taylor Himself	1
Male Slave	1

White Men: Malcom Munroe Himself	1

White Men: Duncan Campbell & two Whites	
	3
Male Slave	1

White Men: Neal McNickals Himself	1

White Men: Mordoch McLoud Himself	1

White Men: Daniel Paterson Himself	1

White Men: John Rosher Himself	1

White Men: Ruben Rosher & two sons	3

White Men: David Rosher Himself	1

White Men: Jesse Moss Himself	1

White Men: Turtle McNeal & son	2
Male Slaves	1
Female Slaves	1

White Men: Daniel McLaughlen	1

White Men: Levy Glass two	2
Male Slaves	1
Female Slaves	2

White Men: Joseph Thims four Whites	4
Male Slaves	2
Female Slaves	1

White Men: John Berry Himself	1

White Men: John Gilcrease	1

White Men: Thomas Jackson	1

White Men: Archibald Little	1

White Men: Neal Thomson	1

White Men: John McCrayney	2
Male Slaves	1

White Men: Alexander Grimes	2

White Men: Duncan Little	1

White Men: Daniel McAfee	1

White Men: Lewis Munroe	1
Male Slaves	1

White Men: Gilbird Ramsey & son	2

White Men: Daniel McAtagar	1

White Men: Absalom Legett	1

White Men: Henry Mercer	2
Male Slaves	1
Female Slaves	1

Dorthity Ikner	
White Men	0
Male Slave	1

White Men: Brittain Barns	1

White Men: Isaac Canadey	1

White Men: William Ard	1
Female Slave	1

White Men: Thomas Creel	1

White Men: Benjamin Britt	1

White Men: Josiah[?] Powel & son	2

White Men: John Little	1

White Men: William Blue	1

White Men: Neal Brown	1

White Men: John McFarson	4
Male Slaves	2
Female Slaves	2

White Men: Uriah Lambardson	1

White Men: George Young	1

White Men: Jesse Musselwhite	1

White Men: Christopher McKay	2

White Men: Absolem Etheridge	1

White Men: William Milen	1

White Men: Daniel McSwain	1

White Men: Robert Sims	1

White Men: Sampson Carver	1
Male Slaves	2
Female Slaves	1

White Men: Robert Upton	1

White Men: Richard Elwell	1

White Men: William Barlow	2

White Men: John Smith	1

White Men: James Smith	1

White Men: James Bigs	1

White Men: Isaac Rosher	4

White Men: John Smith Junr.	1

White Men: John Dorman	1

White Men: Isaac Wilks	1

White Men: Brittain Branch	1

White Men: Samuel Canady	1
Male Slaves	1
Female Slaves	1

White Men: Samuel Canady Junr.	1

White Men: Tobias Seala[?]	1

White Men: James McNeal	1
Male Slaves	2
Female Slaves	1

White Men: David Upton	1

White Men: Malcum Boie	1

White Men: Neal McNeal	1
Male Slaves	1
Female Slaves	1

White Men Alexander McLoud	1

White Men: William Butler	2

White Men: Malcum McNeal	1

White Men: Hecter McNeal Sailor	1

White Men: Neal Brown	2
Male Slaves	1

White Men: Daniel Campbell	1

White Men: Hugh Brown	1
Male Slaves	1

White Men: Anguis Brown	1

White Men: John Newberry	2
Male Slaves	2
Female Slaves	1

White Men: Daniel McEacharn	1

White Men: Milby Musselwhite	1

White Men: Hugh McCrayney	3
Male Slaves	1
Female Slaves	1

White Men: John Baxley	2

White Men: William Smith	1

White Men: John Ward	1

White Men: John Lock & son	2
Male Slaves	2
Female Slaves	3

White Men: James Ellis	1
Male Slaves	5
Female Slaves	1

White Men: Abel Corbet	1

White Men: Jesse Newberry	1
Male Slaves	
Female Slaves	4

White Men: John Newberry Senr.	1
Female Slave	1

White Men: William Lee	1

White Men: Thomas Bud	1

White Men: William Dunn	1

White Men: Gutteridg Lockeleer	1

White Men: Gilbird McCormach	1

Chapter 6:   Bladen County Tax Lists of 1774

White Men: John McCormach   1

White Men: Archibald McCormach   1

White Men: Edward Haley & son   2

White Men: Isaac Lamb & two sons   3

White Men: Thomas Adkison   1

White Men: Joseph Cooper   1
Male Slaves   1
Female Slaves   1

White Men: James McDaniel   2
Male Slaves   2
Female Slaves   1

White Men: William Brumble   1

White Men: James Pate   1

White Men: Thomas Starling & son   2

White Men: Ambrouse Bullard   1

White Men: Thomas Russel   1

White Men: Noah Mercer   1

White Men: John Mercer & John Mercer   2

White Men: James Jackson   1
Male Slaves   1

White Men: Ralph Regon   1

White Men: Henry Taylor & son   2

White Men: Abram Paul   1

White Men: Dempsey Fiveash & John Fiveash
                                         2

White Men: Daniel McLain & John McLain2

White Men: William Wilkison   1

White Men: James Wilkison   1

White Men: William Wilkison Sinr.   1

White Men: James Moore   1

White Men: Arthur Lamb   1

White Men: Simon Cork & James Pierey   2

White Men: Gilbird Cox & John Cox   2

White Men: Joel Pittman   1

White Men: Jesse Pittman & Lot Pittman   2

White Men: Thomas Ivey   1

White Men: Isham Ivey   1

White Men: Benjamin Willis & three Sons 4
Female Slaves   2

White Men: Leonard Lock   1
Male Slaves   1
Female Slaves   1

White Men: Absolem Collings   1

White Men: George Willis   1

White Men: William Thomson   1

White Men: Hardy Inman & two Whites   3

White Men: Alexander McDaniel & two sons
                                         3

White Men: Thomas Pittman & son   2
Molato Slave   1
Female Slaves   1

White Men: Daniel Willis & son also Moab
Stephens   3
Male Slave   1

White Men: James Riseng   1

White Men: Ralph Howel   1

White Men: Thomas Townsend & son   2

White Men: Charles Thomas & son   2
Female Slaves   1

White Men: Charles Bullock   1

White Men: Abram Barns   1
Male Slaves   1
Female Slaves   1

White Men: John Smith   1
Male Slaves   11
Boys   2
Female Slaves   11

White Men: Samuel Smith   1
Male Slaves   1
Female Slaves   2

White Men: Agerton Willis   4
Male Slaves   16
Female Slaves   11

White Men: William Lamb   1

White Men: Archebald McKissek 2
Male Slaves   2
Female Slaves   1

White Men: William Tolar   1

White Men Tarlow Oguinn   2

White Men: Tarlow Oguinn Junr. 1

White Men: Hardy Oguinn   1

White Men: Joseph Melton   1

White Men: Sampson Pittman   1

White Men: Lamuel Britt   1

White Men: Richard Chesher & son & John
Stone   3

White Men: Josiah Handon   1
Male Slaves   3
Female Slaves   1

White Men: Benjamin Sims   1

White Men: Nathaniel Richardson & Samuel
                               2
Male Slaves   5
Female Slaves   1

The Widow Corbet
White Men   1

****

BLADEN COUNTY TAX LIST OF 1774

This List taken for the year 1774   P   Wm.
McRee

Headings for this list include: White Men,
Negroe Fellows, Wenches, Boys & Girls &
Total.

White Men: Thos. Robeson Senr. & Joseph
Moot   2
Negroe Fellows   3
Wenches   5
Boys & Girls   2
Total   12

White Men: Thos. Robeson Junr. & John [?]
                               2
Negroe Fellows   8
Wenches   3
Total   13

White Men: Thos. Owen & Archibald Campbell
                               2
Negroe Fellows   11
Wenches   5
Total   18

Jean Bryan
White Men   0
Boys & Girls   1
Total   1

White Men: John Owen, James Eagerson &
John McBride   3
Negroe Fellows   7
Wenches   4
Total   14

White Men: Robt. Wells & Duncan Gorgam[?]
                               2
Negroe Fellows   2
Wenches   1
Boys & Girls   1
Total   6

White Men: John Roberts & Rickam Reddin
                               2
Total   2

White Men: Joseph Cain   1
Negroe Fellows   2
Wenches   1
Total   4

White Men: John Everitt   1
Total   1

Chapter 6: Bladen County Tax Lists of 1774

White Men: Levi Young, Joseph Appley &
Josua Foreman 3
Negroe Fellows 1
Wenches 1
Total 5

White Men: Thos. Kinlaw 1
Total 1

White Men: Matturin Colvill 1
Negroe Fellows 11
Wenches 12
Boys & Girls 2
Total 26

Margaret Byrn
White Men: James Moore 1
Negroe Fellows 3
Wenches 4
Boys & Girls 2
Total 10

White Men: Daniel McKinzey 1
Total 1

White Men: James Evers 1
Total 1

White Men: John King 1
Negroe Fellows 1
Boys & Girls 1
Total 3

White Men: Matt. Muns 1
Total 1

White Men: Wm. Moorehead & James
Moorehead 2
Negroe Fellows 1
Wenches 1
Total 4

White Men: Jacob Gytan & Richd. Thomas 2
Negroe Fellows 2
Total 4

White Men: Wm. Kirkpatrick 1
Negroe Fellows 1
Wenches 1
Total 3

White Men: John Moore 1
Total 1

White Men: James Counsell 1
Negroe Fellows 2
Wenches 3
Total 6

White Men: Peter Robeson 1
Wenches 1
Total 2

White Men: Peter Byrn, Laurance Byrn, Matt
Byrn & James Moore 4
Total 4

White Men: James Farquson and son John 2
Total 2

White Men: John McNiel 1
Total 1

White Men: James Washburn, Edmd. Chansey
& John Thomas 3
Total 3

White Men: Robt. Baker 1
Negroe Fellows 1
Total 2

White Men: John Cain 1
Negroe Fellows 1
Total 2

White Men: Wm. Cain 1
Negroe Fellows 5
Wenches 4
Total 10

White Men: James Baley, Francis Child &
James Smith 3
Negroe Fellows 6
Wenches 2
Total 11

White Men: Solomon Messer 1
Negroe Fellows 1
Total 2

White Men: Solomon
Messer Junr. 1
Total 1

White Men: Samuel
Andrews, Absolam Ess,
John Andrews & Ruben Roberts Junr. 5
Total 5

White Men: John Oadam, William & Aaron
Oadam   3
Total   3

White Men: Peter Lord, Wm Lord, Wm Wishart
& Thos. Moore   4
Negroe Fellows   3
Wenches   2
Total   9

White Men: John Storm   1
Total   1

White Men: John Caid   1
Negroe Fellows   1
Wenches   2
Total   4

White Men: Anguish Cameron   1
Total   1

White Men: Wm. Groom   1
Total   1

White Men: Jos. Wood Patterool   0
Negroe Fellows   1
Total   1

White Men: Philip Wood Constable   0
Negroe Fellows   1
Total   1

White Men: John Sizmore   1
Total   1

White Men: Even Ellis   1
Negroe Fellows   1
Wenches   1
Total   3

White Men: John Turner & Simon Johns   2
Negroe Fellows   6
Wenches   5
Total   13

White Men: Nathan Horn   1
Total   1

White Men: Edwd. Grantham   1
Negroe Fellows   1
Total   2

White Men: James Grantham   1
Total   1

White Men: Samuel Sutton, Ralph Sutton &
James Parker   3
Total   3

White Men: Richd. Salter, Philip Mattocks,
Edwd Fowler & James Fason   4
Negroe Fellows   2
Wenches   1
Total   7

White Men: Samuel Cain & James Cain
Constable   1
Negroe Fellows   1
Total   2

White Men: John Fowler   1
Total   1

White Men: Josiah Handen   1
Negroe Fellows   3
Wenches   1
Total   5

White Men: John Fasi[?]   1
Total   1

White Men: Johnas Gadin   1
Total   1

White Men: Isaac Sims, James Sims & Elias
Stone   3
Negroe Fellows   2
Total   5

White Men: James Richeson, Jonathan
Richeson & Phil. Ferrel   3
Negroe Fellows   5
Wenches   4
Total   12

White Men: Thos. Scrieven   1
Total   1

White Men: Peter Yeats & Edmund & John
Yeats   3
Total   3

****

BLADEN COUNTY TAX LIST OF 1774

**A List of the Sundry persons taken by James
Bailey for Archibald McKissacks district On
Drowning Creek, 1774**

Chapter 6: Bladen County Tax Lists of 1774

Headings in this list include: Whites, Mix Blood, Men Slaves, Women Slaves & Total.

Whites: Thomas Ard for self and Father   2
Men Slaves: Negro fellow Named Simon   1
Women Slaves: Wench Nan   1
Total   4

Whites: Stephen Glain for self   1
Women Slaves: Negro wench Gin   1
Total   2

Mix Blood: *Jesse Brook (Married) for self & Daniel Dolvin*   2
Total   2

Whites: Charles Barker for self   1
Total   1

Whites: Moses Butler for self   1
Total   1

Mix Blood: *David Braveboy & Wife and Daughter*   3
Total   3

Whites: David Barefield, Self & Thomas Low   2
Total   2

Whites: Miles Barefield, Self, Ezekiel Coward & James Barefield   3
Total   3

Whites: John Blount, Self, Jos Williams & John Smith   3
Men Slaves: Negro fellow named York   1
Total   4

Whites: Jacob Blount for Self   1
Total   1

Whites: James Blount Self   1
Total   1

Whites: Philip Blount Self   1
Total   1

Whites: Joseph Baggett Self   1
Total   1

Whites: Edmund Brown Self   1
Total   1

Whites: Charles Barefield Self   1
Total   1

Whites: Thomas Brown Self   1
Total   1

Whites: Dempsey Barefield   1
Total   1

Whites: William Bird Self   1
Total   1

Whites: Lazarus Creel, Self & Son Lazarus   2
Total   2

Mix Blood: *Cannon Cumbo for self Married*   1
Total   1

Mix Blood: *Ishmall Chivers, Self Married*   1
Total   1

Whites: Roberet Clyvell for self (Say Clyburn)   1
Total   1

Whites: James Carter, Self and 2 Sons Isaac & James   3
Total   3

Whites: William Clapps Self   1
Total   1

Whites: John Dunbar Self   1
Total   1

Whites: Samuel Denn[?]   1
Total   1

Whites: William Edwards Self   1
Total   1

Whites: Samuel Edwards Self   1
Total   1

Whites: Joseph Fort Self   1
Men Slaves: Negros Jacob & Harry   2
Women Slaves: Catt, Moll, Jude & Celia   4
Total   7

Whites: Benjamin Freeman   1
Total   1

Whites: Edward Flowers, Self & 3 Sons John, Drury, Arick & William Barrett   5
Total   5

Chapter 6:   Bladen County Tax Lists of 1774

Whites: William Farrell Self	1
Total	1

Whites: Isaac Groom for Self	1
Total	1

Whites: Andrew Griffin, Self & 2 Sons James & Andrew	3
Men Slaves: Fellow Named Tull	1
Total	4

Whites: Richard Grantham Self	1
Total	1

Mix Blood: *John Hamons for self and wife*	2
Total	2

Whites: George Harrell Self	1
Total	1

Whites: Jesse Harrell, Self and son	2
Mix Blood: *Jacob Mangum*	1
Women Slaves: Girl Named Dandy	1
Total	4

Whites: Elisiah Harrell Self	1
Men Slaves: Negro Sam	1
Women Slaves: Phillis & Violet	2
Total	4

Whites: Humphrey Chambers, Self	1
Total	1

Whites: Thomas Jackson Self	1
Total	1

Mix Blood: *Adam Ivey, Self & Brother*	2
Total	2

Whites: Lewis Jenkins Self	1
Total	1

Mix Blood: *Thomas Ivey*	1
Total	1

Whites: John Jackson Self	1
Total	1

Whites: William Jones Self	1
Total	1

Mix Blood: *Thomas Kersey, Self & William Horn*	2
Men Slaves: Quash	1
Total	3

Mix Blood: *Peter Kersey* Self	1
Total	1

Whites: Thomas Little, Self & Two Sons William and Jesse	3
Total	3

Whites: Shaderic Lee, Self & Father	2
Total	2

Mix Blood: *Jacob Lockelier, Self (Married) & Riding Kersey*	2
Total	2

Mix Blood: *William Lockelier, Self (Married)*	1
Total	1

Mix Blood: [Torn] [Torn]	

Whites: Archibald McLain Self	1
Total	1

Whites: Thomas Musslewhite Self & son Nathan	2
Men Slaves: Negro Harry	1
Total	3

Whites: Malaciah Mercer Self	1
Total	1

Whites: Daniel Maclain Self	1
Men Slaves: 1 Fellow	1
Women Slaves: 1 Wench	1
Total	3

Whites: Joseph Mercer Self	1
Men Slaves: George	1
Total	2

Whites: Joshua Mercer Self	1
Total	1

Whites: John Macdonald Self	1
Total	1

Whites: William Moore Self	1
Total	1

Whites: Sampson Pope Self	1
Men Slaves: Luke	1
Women Slaves: Beck	1
Total	3

Whites: Henry Pope Self   1
Women Slaves: Negro wench Tock   1
Total   2

Whites: John Phillips Self   1
Total   1

Whites: John Rowland Self   1
Men Slaves: George   1
Women Slaves: Phillis   1
Total   3

Whites: James Rowland, Self & 4 sons James,
Wm., Nathn. & Saml.   5
Total   5

Whites: John Regan, Self & James Moore   2
Total   2

Whites: Joseph Regan, Self   1
Men Slaves   3
Women Slaves   2
Total   6

Whites: Whites: Richard Smith for self   1
Women Slaves   2
Total   3

Whites: John Starling, Self & Joel Wells   2
Women Slaves: Bess   1
Total   3

Whites: Thomas Smith and his son Joseph   2
Total   2

Whites: Jonathan Taylor, Self & son William
                                                          2
Total   2

Whites: Benjamin Thomas Self   1
Total   1

Whites: John Wilson, Self & Nicholas
Hervey[?]   2
Total   2

Whites: Joseph Williams, Self given in by Thos.
Ard   1
Total   1

Whites: Edmund Winfield Self   1
Total   1

Whites: Joseph Oates Self   1
Men Slaves: Anthony & Pender   2
Women Slaves: April   1
Total   4

Whites: Carraway Oates Constable   0
Total   0

Mix Blood: *Benjamin Ivey*, Self   1
Total   1

Whites: Thomas Rowland, Self   1
Total   1

Whites: Zackeriah Lee, Self   1
Women Slaves: Deborah   1
Total   2

Mix Blood: *Elisha Sweetin, Self and Son*   2
Women Slaves: two negro Wenches   2
Total   4

Whites: Lewis Hall, Self & Two Sons, Isaac &
Lewis   3
Total   3

Whites: Enock Hall   1
Total   1

Whites: Isaac Hall   1
Total   1

Whites: Joseph Hopkins   1
Total   1

Whites: Joseph Edwards   1
Total   1

Whites: William McFatter   1
Total   1

Whites: John Faisley & his 2 Sons Archibald &
Alexander   3
Total   3

Whites: John Watson   1
Total   1

Whites: Malcom McFatter   1
Total   1

Mix Blood: *James Lowery, Self & wife*   3
Men Slaves: Fellow Jack   1
Total   4

Whites: Thomas Groom for Self	1
Total	1

Whites: Jacob Alford	1
Men Slaves: Boy Hardy	1
Total	2

Whites: Archibald Smith for Self	1
Total	1

Whites: John Best, Self and Brother Bryan Best	
	2
Total	2

Appendix A

APPENDIX A

THE STATE RECORDS OF NORTH CAROLINA
VOLUME XXIII., 1715-1776
EDITED BY: WALTER CLARK
NASH BROTHERS BOOK AND JOB PRINTERS
GOLDSBORO, NORTH CAROLINA, 1904

CHAPTER XLVI.

1715. An Act Concerning Servants & Slaves. (Repealed by Act 4 April, 1741, ch. 24.). (Pages 62-66)

XVI. And Be It Further Enacted By the Authority aforesaid that no White man or Woman shall Intermarry with any Negro, Mulatto or Indyan Man or Woman under the Penalty of Fifty Pounds for each White man or Woman.

XVII. And Be It Further Enacted that no Clergyman, Justice of the Peace or other person licensed to marry shall hereafter presume to celebrate such marriage under the like Penalty of Fifty Pounds for every such marriage one half to the Informer & the other half to be lodged in the hands of the Governor or Commander in Chief for the time being to be applied for & towards the building of any Publick Church, Court-House or Bridges as the Governor shall think fit, and in case no such building shall require it then to the Lords Proprs. to be recovered as is hereafter in this Act appointed.

THE STATE RECORDS OF NORTH CAROLINA
VOLUME XXIII., 1715-1776
EDITED BY: WALTER L. CLARK
NASH BROTHERS BOOK AND JOB PRINTERS
GOLDSBORO, N.C., 1904

CHAPTER V.

1723. An Act for an additional Tax on all free Negroes, Mulattoes, Mustees, and such Persons, Male and Female, as now are, or hereafter shall be, intermarried with any such Persons, resident in this Government. (Pages 106-107).

I. Whereas Complaints have been made by divers Freeholders and other Inhabitants of this government, of great Numbers of Free Negroes, Mulattoes, and other Persons of mixt Blood, that have lately removed themselves into this Government, and that several of them have intermarried with the white Inhabitants of this Province; in Contempt of the Acts and Laws in those Cases made and provided:

II. Be it therefore Enacted, by his Excellency the Palatine, and the rest of the true and absolute Lords Proprs. of Carolina, by and with the Advice and Consent of the rest of the Members of the present General Assembly, now met at Edenton, for the North East Part of the said Province, and it is hereby Enacted, by the Authority of the same, That all free Negroes, Mulattoes, and other Persons of that kind, being mixed Blood, including the Third Generation, who are, or hereafter shall be, Inhabitants or Residents in this Government, both Male and Female, who are of the age of Twelve years and upwards, shall, from the Ratification of this Act, be deemed and taken for Tithables, and as such each and every of them shall, Yearly, pay the same Levies and Taxes as the other Tithables Inhabitants do, and shall, and are hereby made liable to pay the same Yearly to such Person or Persons, in such Manner, and at such Times and Places, and to be subject to such Fines and Penalties, as in and by an Act, intituled, An Act for making the sum of Twelve Thousand Pounds Public Bills of Credit, for exchanging such of the Public Bills of Credit as are now current, thereby to render them the more useful to the Government; and for regulating the Taxes; which the other Inhabitants of this Province, being Tithables, are obliged and subject to.

III. And be it further Enacted, by the Authority aforesaid, That from and after the Ratification of this Act, any White Person whatsoever, Male or Female, Inhabitant of this Government, or that may or shall remove themselves hither from other Parts, that now is, or hereafter shall be, married with any Negro, Mulatto, Mustee, or other Person being of mixed Blood, as aforesaid, shall be, and are hereby made liable to the same Levies and Taxes, as the Negroes, Mulattoes, or other mixed Blood, as herein above is expressed; and it is the true Intent and Meaning of this Act, that all and every of the aforesaid Tithables removing themselves into this Government, shall pay the Levy and Taxes asessed for the Year they come hither, provided they come before the Tenth Day of June in that Year.

THE STATE RECORDS OF NORTH CAROLINA
VOLUME XXIII., 1715-1776
EDITED BY: WALTER L. CLARK
NASH BROTHERS BOOK AND JOB PRINTERS
GOLDSBORO, N.C., 1904

CHAPTER I.
1741. An Act Concerning Marriages. (Page 160).

XIII. And for Prevention of that abominable Mixture and spurious issue, which hereafter may increase in this Government, by white Men and women intermarrying with Indians, Negroes, Mustees, or Mulattoes, Be it Enacted, by the Authority aforesaid, That if any white Man or Woman, being free, shall intermarry with an Indian, Negro, Mustee, or Mulatto Man or Woman, or any Person of Mixed Blood, to the Third Generation, bond or free, he shall, by Judgement of the County Court, forfeit and pay the sum of Fifty Pounds, Proclamation Money, to the Use of the Parish.

XIV. And be it further Enacted, by the Authority aforesaid, That no Minister of the Church of England, or other Minister, or Justice of the Peace, or other Person whatsoever within this Government, shall hereafter presume to marry a white Man with an Indian, Negro, Mustee, or Mulatto Woman, or any Person of Mixed Blood, as aforesaid, knowing them to be so, upon Pain of Forfeiture and paying, for every such Offence, the Sum of Fifty Pounds, Proclamation Money, to be applied as aforesaid.

Chapter II.
Page 332
1749. "An Act to confirm the several Acts of Assembly of this Province therein mentioned ... "

Page 333
1749. "An Act for restraining the Indians from molesting or injuring the Inhabitants of this Government: and for securing to the Indians the Right and Property of their own Lands."

Page 334
1749. "An Act for an additional Tax on all free Negroes, Mulattoes, Mustees, and such persons, male and female, as now, or hereafter shall be intermarried with any such Persons resident in this Government."

Chapter III.
1749. An additional Act to an Act for obtaining an exact List of Taxables; and for the effectual Collecting as well as all Arrears of Taxes, as all other Taxes, for the future due and payable. (Page 345).

II. "Be it Enacted, by his Excellency Gabriel Johnston, Esq., Governor, by and with the Advice and Consent of his Majesty's Council, and General Assembly of this Province, and by the Authority of the same, That all and every White Person, Male, of the Age of Sixteen Years, and upwards, all Negroes, Mulattoes, Mustees Male or Female, and all Persons of Mixt Blood, to the Fourth Generation, of the Age of Twelve Years, and upwards, and all Persons of Mixt Blood, while to intermarry with no other Person or Persons whatsoever, shall be deemed Taxables: Any Law, Usage, or Custom, to the Contrary, notwithstanding."

CHAPTER VI.
1753. An additional Act to an Act concerning servants and slaves. (Pages 388-390).

I. Whereas by an Act, intitled An Act concerning Servants and Slaves, among other Things, it is provided, that no Slave shall go armed with Gun, Sword, Club, or any other Weapon, or shall keep any such Weapon, or shall hunt or range in the Woods with Gun, upon any pretence whatever, except such Slave oe Slaves who shall have a Certificate, as is in the said Act provided: and whereas the Remedy in the

Appendix A

said Act provided has proved ineffectual to restrain many Slaves in divers Parts of this Province from going armed, which may prove of dangerous Consequence: for Remedy whereof,

II. We pray it may be Enacted, And be it Enacted, by the Honorable Matthew Rowan, Esq., President, by and with the advice and consent of his Majesty's Council, and the General Assembly of this Province, That from and after the passing of this Act, no Certificate shall be signed by any Chairman of any County Court in this Province, allowing any slave to carry a Gun and hunt in the Woods, unless the Master, Mistress, or Manager of such Slave, shall first enter into Bond, with sufficient security, to the County Court, either before, or at the time such Certificate shall be given, for the good and honest Behaviour of such Slave; which Bond may be assigned over to any Person or Persons who shall be injured by such Slave; which Assignee shall and may maintain an Action thereon, and recover such damages as he or she shall or may sustain by such Slave, in any Court of Record in this Province, by Action of Debt, Bill, Plaint, or Information; wherein no Essoign, Injunction, Protection, or Wager of Law, shall be allowed or admitted of.

III. And be it further Enacted, That no slave shall have or carry a Gun in any Plantation where a Crop is not tended, nor more than one in any Plantation where there is Crop tended, nor after Crop is Housed: And the Master, Mistress or overseer of any Slave, with whom shall be found any Gun, Sword, or other Weapon, contrary to the true intent and meaning of this and the before recited Act, shall forfeit and pay, to the person finding the same, the Sum of Twenty Shillings, Proclamation Money; to be recovered by a Warrant before any Justice of the Peace for the County where the Offence shall be committed, any punishment inflicted on the Slave, forfeiture of the Gun, Sword, or other Weapon notwithstanding; unless such Master, Mistress, or Overseer shall by their own Oath, or other Proof, make appear that such Slave carrying a Gun, Sword, or other Weapon, was without their Consent or Knowledge.

IV. And be it further Enacted, That the Justices of each County Court, when and where they judge it necessary, shall divide their respective Counties into Districts, and yearly, at the first Court to be held for their Counties respectively after the first day of May, shall appoint three Freeholders in each District as Searchers, who shall take the following Oath, viz:

I, A.B., do swear that I will, as Searcher for Guns, Swords, and other Weapons, among the Slaves in my District faithfully, and as privately as I can, discharge the Trust reposed in me, as the Law directs, to the best of my power. So help me God.

Which Searchers shall four Times in a Year or oftener if they think necessary, search and examine the Quarters and the other Places where Negroes resort in their District, for any Gun, Sword, or other Weapon, and upon finding any of the said Weapons, are hereby required to seize the same, and convert them to their own use, as by the afore-recited Act is directed.

V. And be it further Enacted, That any Person appointed Searcher as aforesaid, who shall neglect or refuse to act, shall forfeit and pay the Sum of Forty Shillings, Proclamation Money, , to such Person, who shall next succeed him; to be recovered as other Fines in this Act mentioned.

VI. And for the Encouragement of such Searchers faithfully to execute their Office, Be it further Enacted, by the authority aforesaid, That each and every Searcher shall, as to his own Person, be, during the Time of his Continuance in his Office, exempted from serving as a Constable, or upon the Roads, or in the Militia, or as a Juror, and shall not be obliged to pay any Provincial, County, or Parish Tax, of what Kind or Nature soever.

VII. Provided always, That no Person but such as are liable to be appointed Constables, shall be obliged to serve as Searchers; any Thing in this Act to the contrary, notwithstanding.

VIII. And be it Enacted, by the authority aforesaid, That no Slave shall hunt or range in the Woods with a Dog or Dogs, except such as shall have a Certificate for hunting, obtained as in this Act directed: And if any Slave shall be found offending herein, it shall and may be lawful for any Person or Persons to kill and destroy the said Dog or Dogs, and to bring the said Slave before the next Magistrate, who shall on due Proof of his Offence, order the said Slave such Correction as he shall judge reasonable, not exceeding thirty lashes.

IX. And be it further Enacted, by the authority aforesaid, That if any Slave or Slaves shall be killed on outlawry, or shall commit any Crime or Misdemeanor for which, he, she, or they, shall be capitally convicted, the Owner of such Slave or Slaves so outlawed or executed, shall be debarred all claim on the Public for the Value of such Slave or Slaves, and the Justices of the County Court and Freeholders, who shall value the Slave or Slaves so killed, or sit on the Trial of such Slave or Slaves so capitally convicted, shall not make any certificate of the value of the same, unless it shall be made appear, on Motion for such Certificate, by the Owner, or some other Person, that such Slave or Slaves, killed on outlawry, or capitally convicted, shall have been sufficiently cloathed, and shall likewise have constantly received, for the preceeding Year, an Allowance not less than a Quart of Corn per Diem.

      X.   And be it Enacted, by the authority aforesaid, That in case any Slave or Slaves, who shall not appear to have been cloathed and fed according to the Intent and Meaning of this Act, shall be convicted of stealing any Corn, Cattle, Hogs, or other Goods whatsoever, from any Person not the owner of such Slave or Slaves, such injured Person shall and may maintain an Action of Trespass against the Master, Owner, or Possessor of such Slave, in the General or County Court, and shall recover his or her Damages, with Costs of Suit; any Law, Usage, or Custom, to the contrary notwithstanding.

THE COLONIAL RECORDS OF NORTH CAROLINA
VOLUME V., 1752-1759
EDITED BY: WILLIAM SAUNDERS
JOSEPHUS DANIELS, PRINTER TO THE STATE

8 JANUARY 1755
(Page 295).
The petition of sundry Inhabitants of the Counties of Northampton, Edgecombe, and Granville was read setting forth that by the laws now in force free negroes and Mulattoes Intermarrying with white women are obliged to pay taxes for their wives and Families Praying Relief and on which the House Resolved that the Matters in the said petition contained are reasonable and that the Committee appointed to Revise the Laws receive a Clause or Clauses to be inserted in the said Laws for their Relief.

THE STATE RECORDS OF NORTH CAROLINA
VOLUME XXIII., 1715-1776
EDITED BY: WALTER L. CLARK
NASH BROTHERS BOOK AND JOB PRINTERS
GOLDSBORO, N.C., 1904

CHAPTER II.
1760. An Act for obtaining an exact List of Taxables, and for the effectual collecting all Taxes for the Future due and payable, and other Purposes therein mentioned. (Pages 526-527).
      I.   Whereas it appears, by the List of Taxables delivered in by the Magistrates at the several and respective Counties of this Province, that a full and compleat List has never yet been obtained by any Law now in Force; and whereas the equal Payment of Taxes is of great Consequence; therefore;

      II.   Be it Enacted by the Governor, Council, and Assembly, and by the Authority of the same, That all and every white Person, Male, of the Age of Sixteen Years and upwards, all Negroes, Mulattoes, Mustees, Male and Female, and all Persons of Mixt Blood to the Fourth Generation, of the age of Twelve Years and upwards, and all white Persons intermarrying with any Negro, Mulatto, Mustee, or other Person of Mixt Blood, while so intermarried, and no other Person or Persons whatsoever, shall be deemed Taxables; any Law, Usage, or Custom, to the contrary notwithstanding.

NORTH CAROLINA STATE ARCHIVES
GENERAL ASSEMBLY SESSIONS RECORDS
COLONIAL (UPPER AND LOWER HOUSE) BOX 2
FILE MARKED (LOWER HOUSE PAPERS)
9 NOVEMBER 1762

To the Worshipful the Speaker and Gentleman of the Assembly:
The petition of Sundry of the Inhabitants of the Counties of Northampton Edgecombe and Granville.
Humbly sheweth,
      That by an Act of Assembly passed in the Year 1723 Intitled "An Act for an Additional Tax on all free Negroes, Mulattoes, Mustees and such Persons Male and Female, as now are or hereafter shall be intermarried with any such Persons resident in this Government." Amongst other Things it was enacted That all free Negroes &C that were or shou'd thereafter be Inhabitants of this Province Male & Female & being of the Age of twelve Years & upwards shou'd be deemed Tythables and as such should Yearly pay the same Levies and Taxes as other Tythable Inhabitants.   That many Inhabitants of the sd. Counties who

are Free Negroes & Mulattoes and Persons of Probity & good Demeanor and cheerfully contribute towards the Discharge of every Public Duty injoined them by Law. But by reason of being obliged by the sd. Act of Assembly to pay Levies for their Wives and Daughters as therein mentioned and greatly Impoverished and many of them rendered unable to support themselves and Families with the common Necessaries of Life. Wherefore your Petitioners would humbly pray in behalf of the sd. Free Negroes &C. That so much of the said recited Act as compels such of them as Intermarry with those of their own complection to pay Taxes for their Wives and Daughters may be repealed Or that they may be otherwise relieved as to your Worships in Your great Wisdom soon.

And your Petitioners as in Duty bound shall pray &C

Granville County

Willm. Eaton
Phil Hawkins
Thos. Lowe
Patrick Lashley
Fras. King
Aaron Fussel
Tho. Dulaney
Zack Bullock
John Williams
John Gibbs
Thos. Hampton
Moses Coppock
Wm. Johnson
Jona. Parker
Richd. Harris
Amus Newsum
Shurley Whately
John Martin
George Jordan

Jno Sallis
Phil Pryor
Jno. Bowie
John Wade
George Buttler
William Falkner
John [?]
Thomas Woodliff
Marton Dickson
Amanuel Falkner
Ezekiel Fuller
James Smith
Wm. Smith
Jos. Brantly
James Brantly
Edwd. Young
Jno. Glover
John Hawkins

Edgecombe

Jos. Jno. Alston
Willm. Anderson
Thos. Wood
John Jones

Northampton [?]

John McCand
Benj. Nevill
James Brown
Joseph Strickland
Jacob Strickland
Ebenezer Folsom
William Richerson

John Cheves
John Fish
Wm. Irby
Benjn. Sherrod
Nathan Joyner
Wm: Adams
Richd. McKinne

[The rest of this page is torn off.]

APPENDIX B

GENERAL ASSEMBLY SESSIONS RECORDS
DECEMBER 1773, BOX 6
NORTH CAROLINA STATE ARCHIVES

18 December 1773
Mr. Speaker Gentlemen of the House of Assembly
      I send herewith for your consideration, a representation of Mr. Archibald McKissak, a Magistrate of the County of Bladen, relative to a number of free Negroes and Mulattoes, who infest that County and annoy its Inhabitants.
New Bern. December 18th. 1773.

Jo. Martin
Governors Message
Informing the House
of a Number of free
Negroes &c., Annoying
the Inhabitants of Bladen
1773.

[Editors Note: The following is a notation on the file by one of the state Archivists.]

Dec. 18, 1773   Petitions rejected, etc.
representation of Archibald McKissak re a number of free Negroes, annoying the inhabitants of Bladen Co. (governor's message only.) (tabled). and list of mob
(List was temporarily stored with the Bladen County Miscellaneous Records from ca. 1959 to November, 1988.)
A List of the Rogues
A List of the Mob Raitously Assembled together In Bladen County October 13th 1773
1. Captain James Ivey
2. Joseph Ivey
3. Ephraim Sweat
4. William Chavours Clark   Harbourers of the
   Commonly Called Boson Chevers   Rogues As follows
5. Richd Groom   Major Lockelear
6. Bengman Dees   Richer Groom
7. Willm. Sweat   Ester Cairsey
8. George Sweat
9. Bengamin Sweat
10. Willm. Groom Senr.
11. Willm. Groom Junr.
12. Gideon Grant
13. Thos. Groom
14. James Pace
15. Isaac Vaun
16. [Torn] Stapbleton
17. Edward Lockelear
18. Ticely Lockelear
The Above List of Rogues is all free Negroes and Mullatus living upon the Kings Land

APPENDIX C

Heads of Households	Total	765
White Males	Total	1088
Mixt Blood	Total	53
Male Slaves	Total	574
Female Slaves	Total	462
Combined Male & Female Slaves	Total	1036

SLAVE HOLDERS WITH TEN OR MORE SLAVES

Mrs. Waddle	70	William Barefoot	14
Thomas McGuire	37	Thomas Brown	13
Agerton Willis	27	John Lucas	13
Berringer Moore	26	James Dupree	11
Maturin Colvill	25	John Owen	11
John Smith	24	Thomas Robeson Junr.	11
Joseph Britton	21	John Smith	11
William Steward	17	John Turner	11
Thomas Owen	16	Thomas Amis	10
John Campbell	16	Walter Gibson	10
William Saltar	14	Thomas Robeson Senr.	10

INDEX

Index

Index

John, 124
Bleu
Wm, 27
Blew
Dugald, 100
Blocker
Wm., 38
Blount
Jacob, 70, 102, 134
James, 102, 134
James Junr., 70
James Senr., 71
John, 70, 102, 134
Philip, 71, 102, 134
Blue
Dougal, 47
Dugald, 62
William, 100, 128
Blunt
Jacob, 6, 14, 43, 80
James, 6, 43, 80
James Junr., 93
James Senr., 93
John, 6, 14, 43, 80, 93
John Junr., 14
Philip, 6, 80, 93
Phillip, 14, 44
Reddin, 93
Boan
Willm., 23
Boazman
Samuel, 66, 75, 101
Bodeford
Mary, 43
Wm., 43
Bodiford
Green, 70, 93
bodyford
Green, 17
Bohand
John, 55
Bohard
John, 28
Boherd
John, 84
Bohodd
John, 28
Boid
John, 73
Boie
Duncan, 100, 127
Malcom, 101
Malcum, 129
Boiy
Duncan, 84
Boon
Archa., 29
Archabald, 94
John, 2
Thomas, 2
William, 2
Bosey

Duncan, 55
Boss
William, 96, 102
Bosswell
Henry, 36
Botchard
John, 100, 128
Boucharty
John, 14
Bourdeaux
John, 126
Bourn
Thomas, 68
Bowie
Jno., 142
Bowman
Ralph, 41, 51
Boyd
Jno., 18
John, 47, 91
John Junr., 47, 62
John Senr., 62, 100
Richard, 52
Richd., 49
Boyets
Jacob, 98
William, 98, 101
Boyte
William, 53, 87
Bozel
Henry, 69
Bozell
Henry, 67
Bozman
Samuel, 90
Bozwell
Henry, 84
Bradly
Archibald, 100
Brafford
William, 19
Braford
William, 65
Branch
Britain, 61
Briton, 95
Brittain, 129
Britton, 33, 101
John, 17, 33, 61, 95
John, Const., 79
William, 79
Brantly
James, 142
Jos., 142
William, 6
Branton
John, 85, 97, 101
John Junr., 97
Samuel, 97
Brantor[Brantford]
John, 69
Braveboy

David, 16, 43, 71, 93, 123, 134
Jacob, 17, 45, 62
Joshua, 8
Lewis, 8
Braveboye
David, 80
Braxton
John, 2
Brazwell
Samuel, 37
Bretford
William, 89
Bridges
Charles, 76
Chas., 90
James, 37
Wm., 86
Briggs
James, 100
William, 81
Bright
[Torn], 10
Richard, 96
Simon, 96, 101
Brigs
Wm., 23
Brit
Nathan, 93
Brite
Buho[?], 39
Richard, 54, 87
Simon, 39, 51, 54, 87
Zacha., 51
Briton
Stephen, 87
Britt
Benj. Junr., 93
Benja., 27, 33
Benja. Junr., 44
Benja. Senr., 94
Benjamin, 82, 100, 128
Benjamin Junr., 70, 81
Jesee, 82
Jesse, 33, 94
John, 8, 82
Lam, 80
Lamuel, 93, 131
Nathan, 33, 81
Samuel, 101
Thomas, an Indian. *See* Indians
Brittain
Stephen, 52
Britton
Joseph, 103, 144
Stephn., 18
Broadas
Peter, 90, 102
Broades
Peter, 74, 126
Broder

C

Index

Index

Index

Index

Index

Index

Index

Index

Index

Index

Index

Index

Index

Index

John, 39
Saml., 86
Potter
Jacob, 42
Miles, 42, 51
Powel
Absalom, 49
Ambrus, 71
Benjamin, 127
Charles, 71, 127
John, 49
John Senr., 49
Josiah[?], 128
powell
Ambrose, 5
Powell
Abram, 42
Absalom, 10, 53
Ambrose, 117
Benjamin, 117
Charles, 117
Isaiah, 30, 56
John, 10, 42, 53
John Senr., 42, 53, 116
Joseph, 117
Josiah, 117
Powers
Joseph, 23, 53, 96, 117
Poynter
Jno, 17
Price
John, 30
Joseph, 30, 57, 62, 127
Pricket
Gidion, 116
Prickett
Gidion, 89
Pridgen
Mathew, 116
Matthew, 126
Procter
Thomas, 35
Proctor
Thomas, 5
Thos., 78
Pryor
Phil, 142
Puff
Andrew, 56, 127
Puff[?]
Andrew, 28
Puffs
Andrew, 117
Purcell
William, 117
Purcey
James, 94
Purkepine
John, 97
Purkins
Joshua, 7
Purnal[?]

Benjamin, 70
Purnall
John, 57
Pusley
Andrew, 30
Putnel
Benjamin, 51
Putnill[?]
Benja., 42

Q

Quarting
Isaac, 82

R

Raborn
Charles, 96
John, 96
Rabourn
Charles, 118
Raiborn
John, 118
Rains
William, 68, 70
Ramsey
Gilbert, 118
Gilbird, 128
Ratleff
Moses, 89
Ratliff
Moses, 76
Ray
Isaac, 21, 87, 118
Joseph, 21, 32, 118
Raybon
Charles, 50, 52
George, 41, 49
John, 11, 42, 50, 52
Raynolds
Richd., 42
Reaves
Nathaniel, 21, 88
Reddin
Rickam, 131
Reeves
Darten, 32
Edward, 75
Edward, Constable, 118
Nathaniel, 32
Regan
John, 71, 117, 136
Joseph, 71, 117, 136
Ralph, 71, 118
Register
Joseph, 50
William, 41, 50, 74
Regon
Ralph, 130

Reives
Edwd., 24
Reve
Nathaniel, 118
Revel
Edmond, 82
Reynolds
Richd., 50
Rhuark
Saml., Const., 50
Samuel, 55
Rial
John, 8
Richards
David, 118
James, 117
Thomas, 117
Richardson
Abram, 16, 79
James, 38
John, 5, 32, 89, 118
John Junr., 21
Nathaniel, 80, 118, 131
Robart, 89
Robert, 32, 117
Samuel, 80, 131
Thomas, 21
Thos., 12, 89
Richerson
William, 142
Richeson
James, 133
Jonathan, 133
Ridget
Richd., 50
Ridgett
Richard, 53
Richd. Snr., 12
Rigan
John, 6, 79
Joseph, 6, 79
Ralph, 6
Richard, 79
Rigel[?]
Richard, 49
Riggan
Ralph, 79
Riggen
John, 14
Joseph, 14
Ralph, 14
Risen
James, 82
Riseng
James, 118, 130
Rising
James, 57
Rivers
Black River, 24
Catawba River, vi
Rivers, 17
South River, 19, 21

164

Index

Index

167

Index

168

Index

Index

Index

www.ingramcontent.com/pod-product-compliance
Lightning Source LLC
Chambersburg PA
CBHW081152270326
41930CB00014B/3124

9780966742503